GIRL
SQUADS

GIRL

SQUADS

20 FEMALE FRIENDSHIPS

THAT CHANGED HISTORY

BY SAM MAGGS

Illustrations by Jenn Woodall

QUIRK BOOKS
PHILADELPHIA

Library of Congress Cataloging in Publication Number: 2017961226
ISBN: 978-1-68369-072-6

Printed in China
Typeset in Verlag and Garamond Premier Pro

Designed by Andie Reid
Illustrations by Jenn Woodall
Production management by John J. McGurk

Quirk Books
215 Church Street
Philadelphia, PA 19106
quirkbooks.com

10 9 8 7 6 5 4 3 2 1

To my own squad

*I feel incredibly lucky to know
so many wonderful and
inspirational women—
your love lifts me up every day*

Contents

POLITICAL & ACTIVIST SQUADS

WARRIOR SQUADS

ARTIST SQUADS

Squad Goals

There are some things you can only text to your best girl friends. You know the ones I mean:

"If your date is bad I'll call you with an 'emergency'"

"Can we see Wonder Woman for a sixth time?"

"I love you but you honestly cannot pull off micro-bangs"

"On a scale of one to ten, how angry should I be at the systemic erosion of my civil rights by the patriarchy"

"Will you come with me to the doc?"

As girls and women, we live in a world that is incredibly difficult to navigate. And although many of us have caring, sympathetic men in our lives, there are some things—no matter how many times we explain them—that they'll never fully understand: what it's like to always wonder if you're being paid as much as the guy at the next desk whose work isn't even as good as yours; how it feels to walk home at night with your keys between your knuckles, wondering if your facial expression is tough enough to scare off assailants but not so tough as to invite aggression; the punch to the gut when someone on the internet threatens you with sexual violence just because you expressed an opinion about a superhero movie. Tell a guy about these and he might just stare at you; tell a gal and she'll *get* it. These shared experiences help us befriend the girls and women around us. They link us with the kind of bond that's impossible to describe unless you've felt it.

Female friendship is a *thing*. So why does TV portray women as catty, competitive, and constantly looking for opportunities to undercut each other? Why do movies often feature a lone "token girl" (if there are any women at all) in an otherwise entirely male cast? What's up with those weird, jealous feelings toward other women that we might get sometimes? And why doesn't the world recognize the amazing power that comes when girls and women team up, bond, and respect one another?

For starters, until very recently, it was the men doing all the writing—men who either didn't think women's stories mattered or, worse, were invested in keeping women in their "place," which meant "apart from one another." A tale of inspiring female friendship was just *too empowering*.

But that doesn't mean those friendships didn't exist. In fact, if we dig deep enough into history, we find that many women who pushed the boundaries and won victories did so because of—and not despite—other women. Who else would cheer them on? The first women to be formally educated, the first women to demand suffrage, the first women doctors—we owe all these success stories to women supporting women. "Girl squads" might be trendy these days (and it's a trend I am 100 percent on board with), but they're not at all new. These trailblazing ladies were the first, and arguably the most important squads of all.

Fortunately, the tide is turning. Everyone is all about the girl squad. Which is awesome, trust me! But it's more than just a solid hashtag (though it also makes a great hashtag). Believing in the strength of women and girls banding together is a shift in consciousness. Promoting positive ideas about female bonding changes how we interact with our own buds. And the magic power of friendship can help us tear down the barriers that are holding us back.

So while society would rather see us compete against each other instead of care about each other, we don't have to listen. We can draw inspiration from historical gals who've lifted each other up and do the same in our own lives. We can connect rather than divide. Because why would we want to talk behind another woman's back when we could compliment her sharp-as-heck winged eyeliner or her new career move and watch her face light up?

The girl squad is about supporting and believing women when they tell us their stories. It's about stopping the fight over the right to be The Girl in the room and insisting that we *all* have a seat at the table—femmes of all ethnicities, races, classes, sexual orientations, gender identities, and abilities. It's about finally getting the women-dominated entertainment and media we are so desperate for (*Ocean's Eight*, anyone?). It's about being more together than we are apart.

So let's rewrite the narrative by seeing how much the amazing girl squads of history have already done. Join me on this journey of lady solidarity, and bring your best girl friends along too.

Oh, and hey—text me to let me know you got home safe, okay? ✦

CHAPTER 1

ATHLETE SQUADS

It wasn't long ago that women couldn't even think about hiking up (or taking off) their skirts to swim, dribble, volley, or ski, let alone dominate these athletic endeavors with their incredibly kick-ass skills. So the groups of women who *did* band together—overcoming discrimination to dominate on the field, in the water, or atop the court—deserve some long overdue recognition (and lots of high-fives). Let's learn more about some of the raddest sporty squads of all time.

The Haenyeo

THE DARING FREE-DIVERS
OF THE KOREA STRAIT

ACTIVE CIRCA 400 AD–PRESENT

Many cultural legends tell of mermaids, supernatural aquatic nymphs with bewitching powers who swim the seven seas. Mythical? Hardly. Mermaids are real, and you can find them a mere hour's flight from Seoul, on the South Korean volcanic island of Jeju. But instead of luring mariners to their deaths or falling in love with sodden princes, these mermaid-like women are amazingly brave (and amazingly skilled) free-divers known as *haenyeo*. And they're even more badass than their mythical counterparts.

A word of Japanese origin, *haenyeo* can be translated as "sea women," and these divers carry on a tradition that dates back centuries. Each morning, they head out across the volcanic island to the rocky shoreline; swim out into choppy, chilly water; dive down over twenty feet; and stay there for around two minutes while they grab sea life by hand. When they resurface, the haenyeo gulp air with a sharp inhale that sounds something like a dolphin—and then they pop back under to do it all over again and again, sometimes up to six or seven hours a day. "Every time I go in, I feel as if I am going to the other side of the world," 75-year-old Yang Jung Sun told *New York Times* reporter Norimitsu Onishi in 2005. "It is all black in front of me. My lungs are throbbing. At that moment I am dead."

It's no wonder the diving feels like death—the women wear no respirators or other mechanical equipment. In fact, they don't have much gear at all, which has been true as far back as records can tell us (i.e., at least a thousand years). Traditionally they wore *mulsojungi* (water clothes) of mega-thin totally-not-protective-at-all cotton to dive unencumbered. Today's haenyeo use glass goggles, rubber flippers, and neoprene wetsuits, which are more protective than cotton—but also more buoyant, making it harder to dive. To offset the extra floatation power, the haenyeo strap themselves into lead-weighted belts, which allow them to sink to the ocean floor. Holding their breath for up to two minutes at a time, they collect abalone, conch, octopus, sea urchins, top shell, and different kinds of seaweed (like the type that gets made into agar-agar for our peel-off face masks), using either their hands or a small metal tool. Thanks to years of experience—the women typically begin diving in their early teens—the haenyeo know exactly which sea creatures will be available where and in what season. They're also careful not to overharvest, so that there will be enough for future harvests (seashell season is from September to May only!). They gather their finds into *taewaks*, hollowed-out orange floaties attached to nets, which resemble the gourds that were used in the past. Then they haul their loads (sometimes over sixty pounds!) onto shore.

Though the tradition dates back generations, these days the haenyeo's work is more grueling than ever. Their wetsuits allow them to stay longer in the water than they could even a half century ago—and most of the women remember those days very well, since the majority of the approximately 2,500 haenyeo are over sixty (!) years old. Oh Byeong-soon, a seventy-seven-year-old with six grandkids, has been diving for over fifty years, including all nine months of each of her pregnancies. The oldest active haenyeo is over ninety, and she still drags in her catches when she can. It's not easy. According to an interview with sixty-two-year-old Yoo Ok-yeon in the *Financial Times*, the women "never know in advance if [they]'re going to die or not," and the nine fatalities over the last five years are proof of that danger.

In 1965, it was predicted that the practice would die out by the end of the twentieth century. But the haenyeo soldier on, their flippers flapping in the ocean waves, because on Jeju, it's the women who bring home the bacon (or the abalone, as the case may be). Around 40 percent of the haenyeo's husbands are unemployed, and their wives' industriousness provides for the whole family. "I can still manage under the sea. My husband had it easy, hardly lifting a finger," Kim Eun-sil, with over sixty years under her lead belt, told the *New York Times*. "Men are lazy," agreed 63-year-old Ku Young-bae. "They can't dive. They are weak under the sea, where it's really life or death."

As you can imagine, this lifestyle, with its unavoidable demands of great strength in the face of adversity (both natural and human-related), has created an inimitable bond among the haenyeo. Before work each day, the women gather in a *bulteok* (fire space), a communal structure by the shoreline that was traditionally made out of low walls of piled-up stones, but now looks more like a regular ol' locker room. There, the women get ready by warming up, helping each other put on their wetsuits, sharing anti-seasickness medication, and just chatting up a storm. Before they head down to the water, you might catch the haenyeo honoring the wind goddess, Yeongdeung Halmang, praying to her for good weather and better fortune. The fully neoprene'd women often get themselves hyped for the day with songs—many of which (probably unsurprisingly) feature tales of female protagonists. One goes

> *Merciful Dragon Sea God,*
> *Although we have good fortune*
> *With abalone and conchs galore*
> *Please let me dive in peace.*

Another talks about children becoming white-haired very quickly; another describes "eat[ing] wind instead of rice" and "tak[ing] the waves as my home" while "the afterlife comes and goes." Dramatic? Sure. But their work is extremely hard.

Out in the waves, and always working in groups, the haenyeo divide their dive locations in different ways; for example, the younger divers swim out farther, and the proceeds of the catch within the designated "School Sea" area aren't kept by the haenyeo but are donated to educational funding. And, of course, there's that wild vocal noise the haenyeo make on surfacing, known as *sumbisori* (which translates as "the vocal sound of the breath," but is also parallel to the word for "overcoming," nice). Passed on from most experienced senior *sanggun* to least experienced junior *hagun* for generations, the *sumbisori* isn't just a cool vocal cue (though the open-mouth, teeth-bearing shape the women's mouths take has no apparent purpose); in fact, it's part of how the divers stay alive. When the haenyeo pop out of the water, they rapidly exhale all the carbon dioxide accumulated in their body, and then they suck in oxygen super-fast, which in turn balances their nitrogen levels and re-expands their lungs. The sound may also help the haenyeo locate one another in the water, even when their vision is blurry. It's tradition, but it's also *science.*

Once diving is complete for the day (a longer shift in summer and a shorter one in winter), these "Amazons of Asia" head back to the *bulteok* and keep working, because their work is pretty much *never* done. After helping one another out of their wetsuits and warming up again, the haenyeo sort and prep their catches for sale, discuss new community policies (like which day that month to skip harvesting and dedicate instead to removing trash from the sea), and train new recruits. Because they dive about fifteen days out of the month, when the tides are weakest according to the lunar calendar, the rest of their time is spent on more traditional land farming, the profits from which they share evenly among themselves. They are a true sisterhood, acting as midwives and caregivers for the elderly, setting up shelters for victims of domestic violence, helping with the Haenyeo School and Haenyeo

Museum, and ensuring their work is as eco-friendly as possible—all this despite only 2 percent of haenyeo in 1965 having a secondary education (many of those haenyeo still being active today). Only then do they go home and take care of their families and prepare to do it all again the next day. Because of their propensity for hard work and their determination in the face of difficult odds, the haenyeo have recently become a symbol of feminism (and, specifically, eco-feminism) in Korea.

Given that they have been at this for centuries, it might be easy to think that the island is a true matriarchy, a regular Themyscira filled with middle-aged mermaids. The truth is more complicated. The diving tradition on Jeju dates back at least one thousand years, but records from the 1600s suggest that initially it was practiced by both women and men. By the 1700s, however, only women were diving professionally. Some historians and scientists who have studied the haenyeo's physiology suggest that the change to a women-only diving tradition might have been due to fat distribution; they reasoned that cisgender women's bodies had relatively more fat and therefore more protection against the cold of the ocean. But other sources dive deeper. As it turns out, more than a few politically motivated forces were at work as well (*quelle surprise*). Among them: a Confucian law prohibiting men and women from diving naked together; another law prohibiting people from leaving the island; super-high "tributes" (read: taxes to the government) imposed on men, to be paid in abalone and seaweed, with corporal punishment for nonpayment; men being conscripted into war or killed in fishing accidents; and the prohibition of island women from marrying mainlanders.

Though it's hard to pinpoint exactly what caused the change, we do know that as soon as the job became "a lady thing," it also became something of a shameful thing. (Like shaming girls for loving One Direction, except directed at female divers and mandated by the Korean government.) From the 1700s until, well, *really* recently, being a haenyeo was not something the women felt proud of. Because their tributes to the Korean government were so high in the 1700s, they felt like state-sanctioned slaves; their husbands weren't even allowed to join the *hyangkyo* (educational circles), damning them to the lowest social tier of manual laborers. Despite consistently being the islands' primary earners (they reeled in 60 percent of the fishing revenue, even into the early 1960s) and bearing responsibility for basically everything good on Jeju, the haenyeo still felt a lot of disdain. (Especially because their thin white diving gear usually left their thighs and shoulders exposed. How scandalous!) Sure, families may have celebrated the birth of girls over boys—but that was only because they knew the girls would be draggin' in that cash. By the 1800s, 22 percent of all women on Jeju Island were haenyeo, earning more through trade with other countries and cultures than men who took factory jobs. But women were never chosen as political leaders, and they were never truly in charge of their own destiny. And since it was a "woman's job," no men ever bothered to learn how to dive, despite knowing that the profession brought in more money than most other occupations.

Nevertheless, these incredible women were not about to let themselves be beat down by the system. It might seem like a dichotomy, but, you know, we contain multitudes and all, and the haenyeo found a sense of personal pride and self-respect from doing work handed down to them through the generations—work they could excel at without formal schooling and that allowed them relatively more control over their lives. (Because the women were the wage earners and had a decent amount of autonomy, Jeju once had the highest divorce rates in Korea.) The haenyeo also banded together to protect themselves and their island. In the 1930s, during Japanese colonial rule of Korea, the women organized a protest against the foreign police after an officer had treated one of their own poorly. They became leaders of the independence movement on the islands and have continued to fight for the preservation of the cultural history of their profession and their home.

And it's totally working—look, we're talking about them right now! Women the world over have taken notice of the haenyeo, holding them up as an example of women's strength and independence in a patriarchal world. And it's a good thing, too, because the current generation of haenyeo just may be the last. In the mid-1900s, their numbers were over 25,000; today, they're down to about 4,000, with only 14 percent under the age of 60. Yet as tragic as that may seem, the haenyeo aren't that broken up about it. They've been able to provide their daughters with educations, jobs, and the *choice* to do what they want. "We are the end," Yang Jung Sun said during her *New York Times* interview. "I told my daughter not to do this. It's too difficult."

Many people now recognize that the haenyeo legacy needs to be conserved—and soon. As a result, scholars and tourists from all walks of life have started dedicating their time and energy to these women divers. Scientists have tested everything from how the women's bodies respond to cold water (better than normal humans, but not as dramatically better now that they wear wetsuits), to how their work affects their bodies in old age, to how their lungs work after years of breath-hold diving. The women have established the Haenyeo Union, part of the Fishery Cooperative Union, which helps maintain the viability of the ecosystem (no scuba tanks = less time underwater = no overfishing). Tourists show up to Jeju on the daily to check out the Haenyeo Museum and to see the women perform their traditional songs. You can even attend the new Haenyeo School to learn the art of diving the sea-woman way (though obviously it takes a lifetime of practice before you can get it right). The Jeju government now pays for the haenyeo's wetsuits, health insurance, and *bulteoks* (now complete with hot water and heated floors!). Most important, in 2016, thanks to the tireless efforts of Lee Sun-hwa—a TV producer, women's rights champion, haenyeo relation and documentarian, and Jeju Special Self-Governing Provincial Council member—the haenyeo were placed on UNESCO's List of Intangible Cultural Heritage of Humanity, ensuring the preservation of their unique and incredible culture for centuries to come.

So don't count them out just yet. The haenyeo were predicted to be gone by the turn of the twenty-first century, yet here they are, still flippin'. And if there's one thing we know about the haenyeo, it's that they have an incredible work ethic. Chae Ji-ae, a 31-year-old who left Jeju to become a hairdresser in Seoul, recently returned to the island to take up the family legacy. "Now I can have free time with my kids, work to the sound of the waves," she told the *Financial Times* in 2015. "There might not be many of us in the future but I don't think we'll disappear completely." Brenda Paik Sunoo, a Korean American journalist who has covered the haenyeo at length, agrees. As she told *Seoul* magazine in 2017: "The sea belongs to all of us. We must go together." ✦

Shirley and Sharon Firth

*THE INDIGENOUS TWIN SISTERS WHO SKIED
THEIR WAY TO THE OLYMPICS*

1953-2013 (SHIRLEY), 1953- (SHARON)

Cross-country skiing is a demanding sport. You need strength, endurance, and the ability to withstand intense cold. You have to keep an eye on your competition. And you have to be able to propel yourself forward using only your own force. Shirley and Sharon Firth did all that *and* had to fight just to get to the starting line. These two women defied the odds, overcoming their circumstances to become two of the most incredible athletes in Canadian history.

Identical twins Sharon Anne and Shirley Anne were born just minutes apart on New Year's Eve 1953, in the tiny hamlet of Aklavik (that's Inuvialuktun for "barren-ground grizzly place"), in Canada's Northwest Territories. (Over one hundred miles north of the Arctic Circle, pretty much due east of the northernmost part of Alaska … it's *cold*, is what I'm saying.) The sisters were close from the start: "We had a really good connection, because, number one, we came from one egg," Sharon said in a 2015 episode of the CBC's *As It Happens*. "All we had to do was give one another a look and we knew what we had to do." Their mother was of Gwich'in (which means "people of the caribou") heritage, and their father, a trapper who hunted caribou, was Loucheaux-Métis (part Athabaskan relative of the Gwich'in, part mixed-race descendant of First Nations peoples and early European settlers). With their ten siblings, the girls were raised as part of the Gwich'in First Nation (although their parents' marriage officially meant their mother had lost her "Indian status" in the eyes of the Canadian government). Though they didn't have much money, their childhood was full of happy memories, living off the land in the tradition of their people. "[Our mother] would take us out to snare rabbits and look at animal tracks," Shirley said in an interview with *Windspeaker* newsmagazine. "Things you don't learn today. It was part of life. That's like how people learned to read books; we were learning to read footprints." The girls learned to fish while their father was on the trapline; that's when their competitive streak first emerged—they argued over whose snares were more successful.

At the end of the 1950s, the Firth family "decided" (i.e., was forced) to relocate from Aklavik to the brand-new town of Inuvik. As in many countries colonized by Europeans, events in Canada followed a predictable, depressing narrative: European settlers, mostly from England and France, were convinced that they alone were "civilized" and that the Indigenous people were definitely not and therefore had no right to their own homeland or culture. To rationalize their takeover of already-occupied lands, the Europeans convinced themselves that, by forcing the Indigenous peoples to abandon their nomadic culture, they were doing "God's work." The colonizers mandated that they use money instead of the buffalo economy, farm instead of track animals, and speak English and French instead of their native languages.

As part of this non-optional assimilation, in 1954 the Canadian government ordered the abandonment and relocation of entire towns, and the Firths' hometown of Aklavik was one of them. The fifty-year-old fur-trading community was thriving at that time, especially in spring after the end of muskrat season; it had two schools, two churches, two hospitals, and familiar hunting grounds for the Gwich'in people. What Aklavik *didn't* have was room for a whole lot of government expansion—and so it had to go. The federal government rattled off reasons for the evacuation (flood risk, no airstrip, poor sewage, no gravel), found a new location (without consulting with the Gwich'in much), and declared Aklavik "sunk." Inuvik was established by the government 35 miles east, designed to be a fully westernized city, complete with lots of new jobs, and by exercising the "option" to move from Aklavik to Inuvik (read: not really optional), even more Indigenous people joined the Western economy. And so the Firths headed to Inuvik (which means "place of man") in 1959, leaving behind the trails they knew so well.

But even after moving, displaced Indigenous families like the Firths were subjected to still more government demands. Residential schools were another even more horrifying method of forced assimilation. Way back in 1884, an amendment to

Canada's Indian Act made school mandatory for Indigenous kids—which sounds pretty okay, maybe even altruistic, until you realize that, of course, ulterior motives were at play. The government realized that getting Indigenous adults to westernize was difficult (people didn't want to just *give up their heritage* because, well, who would?), so officials decided to target children instead. In the 1930s, when the number of so-called residential schools peaked, only about eighty were operating across the entire country. Northern Canada alone is over one million square miles, so a lot of kids would have had no choice but to be shipped off to these underfunded and understaffed institutions that boarded Indigenous kids far from their homes. The schools were filthy and rife with corporal punishment, physical and sexual abuse, and worse.

The distance from home was totally on purpose. The government figured that the farther the kids were from their hometown, the less likely it was that their families would visit them. By attending residential schools, students had little to no contact with their communities, their language, and their culture. But neither did they entirely assimilate after the trauma of being torn from their families. Upon graduation, these students did not fit within Western society *or* their homelands. (The last residential school in Canada closed in *1996—1996*! Twelve years later, Prime Minister Stephen Harper formally apologized for the atrocity on behalf of the Canadian government and ordered a formal report on the schools, which would designate their outcome as a "cultural genocide.")

This was the environment the Firths found themselves in when they relocated to Inuvik and learned their children would be day students at Grollier Hall, the Anglican residential school (from which more than twenty former students would later come forward as survivors of sexual assault committed by school officials). But Shirley and Sharon were lucky, at least a little: after their mother recovered from a brief bout of tuberculosis, which necessitated that the girls board briefly at the adjacent Catholic Stringer Hall, they lived locally with their parents. The girls were fortunate to have family nearby, and in a very right-place-right-time kind of moment, they would also become a part of something called the TEST program.

Despite sounding like a government initiative to create an X-Men-like band of superhumans, the TEST program was actually about creating some kick-ass cross-country skiers (so, okay, maybe not that different), with a little help from the government. Back in the early 1960s, Prime Minister Pierre Trudeau (father of Justin, the hot, tattooed PM elected in 2015) had noticed that, despite the country being about 99 percent snow and ice, Canadians were not performing so well at the Winter Olympics. To remedy this problem (and tend to national pride), his administration established the Task Force on Sport for Canadians (really and truly what it was called!), which recommended that the federal government pour money into communities to develop new fitness initiatives to make Canadian citizens More Good at Sports.

Coincidentally, over in Old Crow, in the far northwestern Yukon Territory, a Catholic missionary priest named Jean Marie Mouchet (who had patrolled on skis with the French Resistance during World War II) was already on top of the "teaching everyone sports" trend, coaching Indigenous kids in skiing. Specifically the cross-country variety, because the terrain wasn't quite right for downhill and because it fit in with the children's traditional overland skills, like hunting and trapping. Father Mouchet also hoped that giving the kids an after-school sport to look forward to might curb their (understandable) delinquency.

In short, money + coaches = teams. Thanks to a grant from the newly sports-crazy government in 1965 (and a donation of skis from the US Air Force, of all places), Father Mouchet was able to expand the scope of his work by establishing the Territorial Experimental Ski Training (TEST) Program out of Grollier Hall (and, later, a big warehouse) in Inuvik. With help from the Canadian Amateur Ski Association, Father Mouchet hired Norwegian ski coach Bjorger Pettersen and began to offer cross-country skiing lessons to children at the local residential schools, in the hopes not only that they would someday become Olympic athletes (although, yes, that), but also that participating in competitive sports might motivate the otherwise traumatized youths to do better in school and in life. "They were trappers, they were hunters," Mouchet said of his charges in 2011, in an interview for the Cross Country Canada website. "They were living in the very cold climate doing ordinary work, like cutting and packing wood and going down to the river to bring water up. It gave them the right components [for skiing]."

For Shirley and Sharon, the TEST program was a huge opportunity, and not just because skiing let them skip church on Sundays. Among the many failures of the residential schools was a lack of athletic opportunities for girls. (One Ontario residential school had a "track and field day," during which girls raced to a vanity, put on makeup and hairpins sans mirror, and ran back. *Yikes*.) But the Firths weren't convinced they should join. They worried about being ostracized for not being Catholic, and their mother had to convince her daughters to try out for the team. The girls were twelve when they skied for the first time, which they did in their jeans. And once they started, they never wanted to stop. "I found [skiing] so wonderful," Shirley told *Windspeaker*. "It was something you could do by yourself and use your own power." Their greatest dream was to travel the world, and they knew this was their best chance.

The twins' coaches quickly recognized their talent. "They didn't have an easy upbringing and were very timid when they first came," said Bjorger to Cross Country Canada. "Of all of the skiers I had they were the most competitive and determined. In Inuvik we often skied at forty-five below zero; their lungs were used to cold weather." Though at first they had no idea how to ski, the girls set their minds to it, using the determination they had learned from trapping and tracking to propel them forward to their goal.

With nearly five hundred skiers based out of Inuvik, the TEST teams started competing. After winning local competitions and making Bjorger's elite team, the Firths headed to their first big competition in Alaska (together, of course). They were sixteen years old and had never flown, never seen a city as big as Anchorage, and found themselves fascinated by elevators and escalators and streetlights. At the competition, they faced off against an American Olympian. "I remember beating her," Shirley told *Windspeaker* in 2006. "Just by a couple of seconds, and it upset her whole lifestyle because it was unheard of—especially by a Native girl. So that was pretty funny! And at the time you don't really think of being Native. Just the way it was. When you're on the starting line there's no color or size or anything, just the one who was the winner."

That win would be prophetic for Sharon and Shirley, who continued to compete hard, winning a combined forty-eight Canadian championships over the course of their careers. In 1972, at the age of eighteen, they became the first Canadian Indigenous women to qualify for the Winter Olympics. Tragically, right before the games started in Sapporo, Japan, Shirley contracted a near-fatal case of hepatitis. "When she was first diagnosed, my biggest fear was losing her," Sharon later reflected to Cross Country Canada. "When I trained I would visualize Shirley beside me, like us skiing together." Fighting the illness, Shirley still managed to compete at the Winter Games, though her performance was not as great as she had hoped (she finished twenty-fourth in the five-kilometer race, setting a Canadian record that stood until 2002—not a bad showing). Together with Sharon, Shirley helped the Canadian three-by-five-kilometer relay team finish in tenth place, setting another national record.

Though the sisters often competed against each other, they didn't let the rivalry bother them: "When you're an athlete you compete against yourself," Sharon told *Windspeaker*, "and as long as you know you've done your training and your homework and your preparation you can't really let the other person race for you. When Shirley won it was good; when I won it was good. We fed off each other." Their friendship held fast as they continued to rule Canadian cross-country skiing for most of the 1970s and 1980s, slaying World Cup and World Nordic championships with a team made up mostly of other kids from the Inuvik TEST program. Sharon and Shirley became the first athletes to represent Canada at four consecutive Olympic games: they competed in 1976 in Innsbruck, Austria; in 1980 at Lake Placid (instead of attending their mother's funeral, knowing it was the best way to honor her memory); and in 1984 in Sarajevo.

However, the constant competition, training, and traveling wasn't easy. "We had to learn a whole new way of life," Sharon told scholar Christine O'Bonsawin in 2002. "Eating habits, being introduced to fast foods, which I think is a crime. Sometimes we starved ourselves because we could not eat the food, and still we raced on." At the time, Shirley often felt like an outsider: "The Russian girls keep asking us about [retired Canadian hockey players] Phil and Tony Esposito," she told the *Toronto Star* in 1976. "Who are those guys, anyway?" When they returned to Inuvik between competitions, they felt isolated there too, belonging fully to neither world. "When we go home now, the kids our own age, our old classmates, seem very strange to us," she said. "I guess we strike them as pretty weird, too. We've become strangers in our own hometown."

The press was not always kind to the Firth girls, either. Coverage often showed prejudice against their Métis and First Nations heritage or disparaged their lack of medal wins without considering the difference between their bootstrap training and the extensive formal preparation of athletes representing other nations. "To be competing with giants at that level was a tremendous accomplishment for us as Aboriginal women," Sharon later told the CBC. "We said, 'if we can do it, anyone can do it.'" Bert Bullock, another Canadian cross-country skier at the 1976 Olympics, later put the Firths' accomplishments into context: "If you want to take the entire Canadian athletic scene into perspective," he told Cross Country Canada, "those two ladies have gone a long way in a short time and through a lot of obstacles. Everything from male chauvinism to prejudice to all the ugly things we deal with today. We went through all that and especially them because they're female and they're aboriginal."

The 1984 Olympics would be the sisters' last, an end they both saw coming. Shirley had married a year before, and they both knew that if one of them retired, then the other would follow suit. In addition, the National Ski Team office had been pressuring them to retire from competition for years, which Sharon suspected was racially motivated. "We didn't win a medal," Sharon told *Windspeaker*, "but the high note was making all those Olympic teams. It was all so good, that is why we lasted so long. We had endurance." They struggled after retiring, with little government support or compensation for all they'd done for their country, but both women eventually found their way, relying on their close bond at every step. Sharon moved back to the Northwest Territories, working as a youth adviser with the NWT government (a decade and a half after she first applied and was rejected for her lack of secondary education—which the Canadian Amateur Ski Association had forbidden her from getting while she was competing). Shirley settled down with her husband in Chirens, France, raising three daughters, earning a teaching diploma from the University of Paris, and lecturing on Dene and Inuit cultures at schools and cultural institutions around Europe. The Ski Association never approached the Firths about becoming coaches, the established career path of many retired Olympic athletes. Despite her incredible achievements, Shirley was reticent to speak about her skiing career, preferring to live a "humble" life with neighbors who knew her simply as "Shirley" and not as "Shirley the Olympic athlete." When she eventually returned to the Northwest Territories in 2005 to teach her curious teenage daughters about their roots, her home was just as she remembered. She told *Windspeaker*: "It's so beautiful, like a dream to see all the trees with white crystals."

Though the TEST program was dismantled in 1984 due to cutbacks, the sisters decided to try to revitalize interest in skiing in the NWT in the 2000s and present themselves as role models for Indigenous youth, even working with CBC Sports on a documentary about their Olympic career. At a 2001 symposium in Inuvik dedicated to the TEST program, Sharon reflected on its ups and downs: "We dreamed about seeing the world, and TEST became the way for us to see our dreams become reality. There was a lot of pain and sorrow, but there were many good times as well." Shirley's husband, Jan Larsson, also reflected on the sisters' accomplishments to the CBC. "They broke a lot of barriers to represent themselves, the Gwich'in, the First Nations," he said. "I hope it will stimulate young Aboriginal youth today to see that if they want it, they can get it." Thanks to writer Sally Manning, the sisters even saw their story published in 2006 as *Guts and Glory*. "Like my sister Sharon says, we are a part of Canadian history,"

Shirley told *Windspeaker* when the book was released. "We're like the explorers. There are not too many people who have done what we have."

After being diagnosed with lung cancer in 2011 (despite never smoking), Shirley still rode her bike every day to her job as executive assistant for a Northwest Territories Legislative Assembly speaker. When she passed away from cancer in 2013, Shirley wanted her message to be one of family, health, and education. Sharon spoke at all the events for their Canadian Sports Hall of Fame induction in 2015, discussing at length the importance of education and sports programs for Indigenous youths.

Over the span of their career, the Firth sisters won national championship medals and set several national records. They were the first Nordic skiers to be honored by the Canadian Ski Association for their contributions to the sport. They were named members of the Order of Canada in 1987, inducted into the Canadian Ski Hall of Fame in 1990, awarded the Queen's Golden Jubilee Medal in 2002, and they became the first NWT honorees of Canada's Sports Hall of Fame. Today, an award named in their honor is presented annually by the national sports organization Cross Country Canada to a woman who has made an "outstanding volunteer contribution" to Canadian cross-country skiing.

Sharon and Shirley Firth came from the harshest circumstances, but despite their challenges, they never stopped fighting for each other. As Sharon said to *Windspeaker*, "There was lots of pressure, but Shirley and I had one another." ✦

The 1964 Japanese Women's Olympic Volleyball Team

THE "WITCHES OF THE ORIENT" WHO DOMINATED THEIR SPORT

ACTIVE 1954–1964

Imagine this: you're on the volleyball court, staring up at one of your opponents, a woman much taller and wider than you. Your hands are bleeding, your shoulder is bruised, and your collarbone feels like it's been broken and rebroken a thousand times. An Olympic gold medal and the future of your country's national identity are on the line. Five of your best and oldest friends surround you, and you know they won't let you down. You can't let them down, either.

That may sound like the opening scene of a feel-good sports movie, but it's not fiction. For the women of the 1964 Japanese

Olympic volleyball team, this make-or-break moment was 100 percent real, and their story more than deserves the big-screen treatment.

To understand why this particular game was more than just a question of who wins the most points, let's get some context. In the years after World War II, Japan was dealing with what you might call an identity crisis. It had lost the war, and in the process the country lost not only soldiers, civilians, and infrastructure but also national pride, after the US forced the Japanese to adopt a free-market capitalist system and instituted a new Western-style constitution. The US occupation of Japan continued until 1952, after which the Americans left and the country was governed by a postwar constitution with strict *no military shenanigans* rules (i.e., Japan lost all its territories and was forbidden from having an army). It was a tough time, and literature from the postwar era tells us that the Japanese people felt embarrassed and hopeless. They desperately wanted to rebuild their economy, their self-esteem, and their international image as quickly and as effectively as possible. A tall order. (And not one you'd think volleyball would necessarily solve—but we'll get to that.)

Japan managed to bounce back from the devastation of the war by getting good at manufacturing cars and technology—*very* good, in fact. By 1965, the people of Japan not only spent more hours watching television (on Japanese-made TVs) than doing literally anything else, but they also watched more TV than any other country in the *world*. This was great not just because TV is excellent, but also because this newly accessible mass medium helped promote a coherent and communal narrative about who the Japanese people were becoming as a nation by providing shared experiences, even across vast distances.

But the postwar boom was about more than just TV. Japan also revived its textile-production industry, which was a big deal because the goods and revenue generated by cotton-spinning factories had helped the country to militarize in the first place. In the mid-twentieth century, textile factories became a massive employer—of mostly low-paid, impoverished, rural women. (Funny how so many economies tend to be built on the backs of unrecognized and underpaid labor by marginalized folks, huh? *Huh?*) Since the early 1900s, poor country families had been sending (read: selling) their daughters to textile factories as a sort of money-making interim between schooling and marriage. Every March, countless girls who had just graduated higher school (around age 18 or 19) would board trains bound for industrial areas, where work—and a whole new life—was waiting for them. Not only did the factories provide employment, but with a paternalistic "we're helping!" mindset they also offered dorm living, on-site food and recreation, and even "suitable" men for the girls to wed. Factory girls went home only twice a year (for New Year's in January and for the August festival of Obon, a traditional celebration of ancestors and family). Their lives were strictly organized and controlled, in large part to, you know, protect their chastity and all that. Overall it was a pretty restrictive system, but it did allow the girls to form super-close friendships and gave them night school opportunities plus lots of extracurricular sports and activity groups—including, yep, volleyball. (Told you we'd get there).

Volleyball had been invented at a Massachusetts YMCA in 1895 by physical education director William Morgan as a simpler alternative to basketball (he originally called it "mintonette," but that just doesn't have the same ring). The sport quickly gained popularity across the globe—especially in poorer communities—because it was cheap to set up and easy to play. All you need is a ball, a little bit of space, and some folks to play—no special equipment or fancy court needed. The modern sport has six players per team (though in pre-1960s Japan teams had nine): three in the front row and three in the back, with a player called the setter running the team's offensive strategy, similar to a quarterback in football or point guard in basketball. The team has to hit the ball back and forth over the net using hands or forearms, sending it sailing from afar or spiking it at high velocity close to the net, until the ball either goes out of bounds (resulting in a point for your opponent) or hits the floor on your opponent's side (scoring a point for you). By the '60s, games consisted of three matches of five sets, each to fifteen points, and were won by a margin of two points.

In postwar Japan, volleyball took off in rural communities, and textile factories were quick to jump on their employees' love for the sport, which provided play space that encouraged friendship, leadership, and discipline. The workers lived together, worked together, and supported one another, so volleyball perfectly complemented the team-building already in place. Kanegafuchi Bōseki (a cotton-spinning operation colloquially known as Kanebō) started the first company volleyball team back in 1913, and by midcentury leagues were competing across the nation—

including at Nihon Bōseki (Nichibō), one of the Big Ten cotton spinning corporations. It was there that a young woman named Masae Kasai would soon begin to work.

The fourth daughter born to a farming family in Yamanashi prefecture, Masae played volleyball all through higher school—at first because she thought the coach was cute, and later because she was darn good at it (not least because she was five-foot-seven, a full seven inches taller than the average Japanese woman at the time). In her final year of school, at age 18, she was scouted for her volleyball skills by a representative from Nichibō, the textile company with the top team in the country. He offered her a spot on the squad, which also meant taking paid work at the factory. Masae thought the whole thing felt "like a dream," as she later told scholar Helen Macnaughtan, and her parents couldn't believe their luck. After graduating in the spring, Masae boarded a train and for the next two years worked at one of the Nichibō locations. In 1954, she was transferred to their Kaizuka factory, just south of Osaka, about three hundred miles southwest of Tokyo. It was there that Nichibō decided to assemble The Greatest Volleyball Team of All Time: Kuniko Tanida, Emiko Miyamoto, Yuriko Handa, Yoshiko Matsumura, and Sata Isobe. All these girls, who came mostly from agricultural families, were recruited to Kaizuka either from other Nichibō factories or straight from school by Nichibō's infamous coach, Hirofumi Daimatsu, better known as Oni no Daimatsu—"Daimatsu the Demon."

As an Imperial Army commander during World War II, Daimatsu fought in the jungles of Burma and New Guinea and survived two years in a British prisoner-of-war camp before being repatriated. Daimatsu had been a volleyball champ in college, but on taking his first postgraduate job at Nichibō, they told him that his time fooling around on the court was over. When he returned to the company after the war, he was met with a surprise: instead of being an afterthought, his volleyball skills were suddenly a huge asset. Nichibō sent Daimatsu to Kaizuka, where he quickly set about finding the best volleyball players at the company's factories and at girls' schools around the country. He was the coach who brought together Masae and what would be her incredible team.

Oh, and Daimatsu was also *terrifying*. The former platoon commander used a form of training that came to be called *satsujin taisō* (which roughly translates to "homicidal training" or "murderous exercise"—either way, *bad*). Though he never used corporal punishment, as the higher school coaches had done, his methods were brutal. Still, his team never said a negative word about him (players often referred to him as their father, brother, and boyfriend all in one: healthy!), but he worked them tirelessly, providing no days off. When they inevitably broke down in tears, he would yell things like, "Well, you might as well just give up, then!" and "If you want to go back to your mother then just go!" He told them to forget they were women and refused to honor the 1947 Labor Standards Act that granted women workers menstrual-leave days. Daimatsu was convinced that the more time the girls spent working as a team, the better they would play.

The girls' days were, in a word, long. They woke up every day around 6 a.m., arrived at their desks by 8 a.m., and worked on clerical tasks until around 4 p.m. From there, it was nothing but volleyball, and hardcore volleyball at that. According to Kuniko, they often practiced for at least six hours before heading back to the dorms to do laundry and wash up before bed. Masae later remembered that her roommates who weren't on the team would make up her bed and leave a hot water bottle between the sheets for her, an act of kindness that encouraged Masae to train even harder to make them proud.

And she and her teammates were already training pretty dang hard. They were no strangers to bloody hands and bruised bodies, and obviously they had no time for a social life: five-foot-six Emiko often joked that she was just waiting to find a man taller than she was, and Masae said they practiced so much that "we forget we are women." In 1957 Masae was made team captain (she said it was because she was the oldest by four years, but, as the setter, she *did* have the ball most often), and within a year the team was ready to run for Japan's four big volleyball titles. The girls started hitting, and they started winning.

But no sooner had they climbed to the top of Japan's volleyball ladder that the Nichibō Kaizuka players started to dream bigger. Because of their corporate sponsorship and reputation as the best in the country, the Japanese Volleyball Association sent them to the World Championships, flying Masae and her teammates all the way to Brazil to compete on the international stage. It was the first time a Japanese women's team was included. The men's team came in eighth. The Nichibō Kaizuka squad placed second. They were bested only by the women's team from the Soviet Union, which was on an eleven-year winning streak.

Suddenly, Nichibō knew they had something special. The

team immediately started to prepare for the next World Championships in Moscow, two years down the road. Daimatsu, whose attitude about sports was "kill or be killed," believed that "second place is nothing." His players began training until past 1 a.m. nightly to improve their skills—but it still wasn't enough. Their coach was convinced they needed something beyond hard work and long hours to put them ahead of other teams, something to help them succeed under even the most difficult circumstances. To aid what he perceived as, shall we say, his team's *short*comings, after watching their loss to the Soviets (whose players were roughly six feet tall), Daimatsu developed new techniques to help the girls move faster and more nimbly on the court. A few were useful, like the *konohaochi sābu* (falling-leaves serve) and the *jikansa kōgeki* (time-lag attack), but Daimatsu and the Nichibō team would be remembered for one move in particular: the *kaiten reshību*, or rolling receive.

Based on a judo move, the *kaiten reshību* required the girls to dive to the floor to defend a spike and then perform a quick shoulder roll to return to the standing defensive position as quickly as possible. Through the entire move, their butts never touched the floor, gaining the athletes precious seconds of play time. If you're thinking this move looked like a bunch of girls repeatedly launching their shoulders to the floor over and over and over and over again until they cried with pain, you would be correct. One *LIFE magazine* reporter called the *kaiten reshību* an "exercise in mass masochism," and *Sports Illustrated* was "chilled by the fanatical striving" of the process.

But dang, did it ever work. Leading up to the World Championships, Kasai and her team toured eastern Europe in 1961, soundly trouncing teams in Bulgaria, Czechoslovakia, Poland, and Romania. Coming off a twenty-two-game winning streak, they rolled into Moscow in October 1962 to face off against the Soviets on their home turf. This time, they crushed it. The *kaiten reshību* was so effective that viewers thought the team was performing "magic tricks," and the Russian newspaper *Nedela* called it a "secret weapon." According to Daimatsu's own account in the book he wrote about the team, the Soviet papers had been calling the Japanese team the "Typhoon of the Orient" until then; after their World Championship victory, the Russian press realized their power was not as fleeting as a storm. The Japanese press quickly latched on to the USSR's new name for the Nichibō team, which echoed Soviet pejoratives for Japanese soldiers during World War II: Чародейка. *Tōyō no majo.* "The Witches of the Orient."

The team returned home to nationwide fervor. Kasai, already 29 years old (and therefore verging on "old maid" age in those days), and a few of her teammates planned to retire after the World Championships, going out on top. But there had been some new developments while the squad had been out of the country: Japan was now set to host the Olympic games in Tokyo just two years later, in 1964—the first Olympics ever held in Asia. Oh yeah, and for the first time in history, women's volleyball was added to the program.

Letters from passionate fans poured in. At a critical rebuilding moment in the country's history, the Japanese people saw the Witches as their opportunity to win gold on the world stage, and they weren't about to let Kasai and her team walk away. Plus, the nation was invested in the Witches' rivalry with the Soviets; Japan and the Soviet Union were not in a great place, diplomacy-wise, having been in conflict for decades, beginning with Japan's defeat of Russia in the Russo-Japanese War of 1905, squabbling over who got to be the biggest imperialists to Manchuria and Korea. World War II and its aftermath also exacted a great toll: the Soviets had captured nearly 600,000 Japanese troops and some islands north of Hokkaido, and in the late 1940s, tens of thousands of Japanese had died in Siberian POW camps. Plus, as Daimatsu liked to point out, the Soviet women didn't work for a living in addition to their training, unlike *his* players. And so, at a post–New Year's gathering in 1963, the Witches decided to do this one last thing, for their team and for their country. And then they got to work.

Ten of the twelve players for the Olympic team were select-ed from the Nichibō team. Masako Kondo from the Kurashiki textiles team and Ayano Shibuki from the Yashica camera com-pany team rounded out the squad, and a year of intensive train-ing began. Meanwhile, Tokyo was preparing for its international debut, desperate to show the world how far Japan had come in such a short time. Huge sections of the city were razed and re-built, and the first *shinkansen* high-speed train roared to life just ten days before the opening ceremonies. Sales of Japanese televisions skyrocketed as people across the nation prepared for the event, which would be broadcast not only via satellite, but in color to boot. Daimatsu assured the press that the team was "witches with good hearts" even though they weren't very pretty (what a guy!), and the press in turn portrayed the women as the embodiment of self-sacrifice, putting the good of the nation before themselves. As noted in *The 75-Year History of Nichibō*, the official "Instructions for Factory Girls" in 1910 referred to female workers as the "flowers of the people." Now, these laborers were called the "flowers of the Games." With their bruised shoulders and bold determination, they were ready.

On October 10, 1964, a student who was born in Hiroshima on the day of the atomic bombing lit the Olympic torch. The Tokyo games were about to begin. Traditions the nation had worked for nearly two decades to mold into symbols of peace (the emperor, the Red Sun flag, the national anthem) were now displayed with pride. By October 23, the day before the closing ceremonies, Japan's athletes were in third place for total medals, behind the US and the USSR. But early in the day they suffered a blow; having fought hard for judo's inclusion in the games, they expected to walk away with gold in the open weight category, only to be bested at the last minute by the Dutch. A defeat in a Japanese martial art was crushing, and the nation's pride was hurting. The last chance for gold would be that very afternoon: the Witches versus the Soviet Union.

The streets of Tokyo emptied. The Nippon Telephone switchboards went dark. More than 85 percent of the country's viewers turned on their TV to witness the fate of their favorite volleyball players. "If we lose, we might have to leave the country," one of the players said nervously as the Witches took center court, with four thousand fans watching from the stands. The Soviets were taller, but the Witches were faster, and they had the *kaiten reshī-*

bu on their side. The game started at 7 p.m. The Witches took the first set, 15 to 11. They took the second set, 15 to 8. And they were leading the third set, 13 to 6—but then the Soviets started to come back. 13 to 7. 13 to 8. 13 to 9. 14 to 9. 14 to 10. 14 to 11. 14 to 12. 14 to 13. The Soviets were now only *one point* behind the Witches.

Daimatsu called a time-out, after which Emiko served, sending the ball soaring over the net. A Soviet player passed it to a teammate standing closer to the net, who reached up to bat it over—but the whistle blew. The Soviet player had reached over the net—an illegal move. And with that, the Witches won Japan's sixteenth gold medal of the games.

The stadium burst into a roar, every person leaping to their feet. Around the country, millions of spectators watching at home did the same. Overjoyed, the Witches leapt into one another's arms. Masae didn't let herself cry "until her mission as team captain finished," but the sense of victory was overwhelming. They'd done it. And in the process they'd helped their country reinvent itself.

The Witches went on to win over 250 consecutive games. Schoolgirls across the country emulated the *kaiten reshibu* until the move was banned after a series of children suffered broken collarbones. The players were hailed as "national heroines," and their win was symbolic in several ways. The *kaiten reshibu* was a hard fall and a quick return, a perfect metaphor for Japan's postwar reconstruction. The Witches had won not by strength, but through a series of clever innovations, just as Japan was doing in manufacturing and technology. They were a group of hardworking, self-sacrificing individuals who had given up everything for the success of their company and their nation, representing ideal citizens. And despite the decidedly less empowering aftereffect of Daimatsu getting the lion's share of the credit for the win, plus the fact that the corporate sports complex was established as a way to control women's postwar social lives (fill their time with volleyball so there's no time for bad behavior, ya dig?), there was no denying that this band of tenacious, tough-as-nails working-class women shepherded Japan toward its future.

The Witches went on to great fame and success in their chosen fields, some retiring immediately to start families, others teaching or starting their own businesses. Sata's son swam in the 1988 Summer Olympics in Seoul. Masae was introduced to a Japan Self-Defense Forces officer by the prime minister, who later gave a speech at their highly publicized wedding in 1965. (Aw!) She eventually became a longtime ambassador for sports, volleyball, and the Olympics in Japan, carrying the torch at the 1998 Winter Games in Nagano. She was inducted into the International Volleyball Hall of Fame in 2008. In 2012, a year before her death, a 79-year-old Masae Kasai recounted that she and the other Witches still kept in touch over the phone and on trips to Osaka. "When we meet up," she said, "it's just like the old days, and we're still all the same. We have a very strong bond." And with good reason: the Witches helped Japan find its spirit and, in the process, discovered their own power too. ✦

Madison Keys and Sloane Stephens

THE TENNIS PRODIGIES
WHO LITERALLY REACHED
ACROSS THE NET

1995– (MADISON), 1993– (SLOANE)

Madison Keys and Sloane Stephens have been hailed as the saviors of women's tennis in the United States, the next generation of American talent following in the footsteps of Venus and Serena Williams in a country-clubby sport that hasn't traditionally been welcoming to women of color. Since Althea Gibson's 1956 victory at the French Open, which made her the first Black person to win a Grand Slam tournament (the four major annual competitions in tennis), Black women players have faced the double difficulty of both gendered and racial discrimination in tennis clubs and competitions. US tennis in general has suffered a drought for the last, oh, several decades; besides the Williams sisters, the

last Americans to win Grand Slam events were Jennifer Capria-
ti and Andy Roddick—in 2002 and 2003, respectively. Which
is all part of what makes Madison and Sloane, rising stars and
best buds, so very extraordinary. What's more, they're living up
to their reputations: in 2017 both advanced to the final match of
the US Open. Against . . . each other.

Why is that so remarkable? Well, team sports and friendship
go pretty much hand in hand. Having close buds is easy when
you're part of a team. Sure, internal strife exists, but at the end
of the day you have a group of girls you know you can rely on,
no matter what. It's y'all against the world. In individual sports,
though? Not so much. All the pressure to succeed falls on your
shoulders alone. With you and your opponent in tight quarters,
there's bound to be tension in the locker room before a big competition, whether it's gymnastics or skiing or swimming. Fortunately, once you're out there, all you have to concentrate on is
your own performance.

Unless, of course, you're staring your competition right in
the eye—like in tennis. When you walk onto the court, it's one-
on-one, you or her. Every point you score, your opponent loses.
Every set she wins is one that you lose. On the other side of the
net stands the Terminator to your Sarah Connor, the Galactus
to your Squirrel Girl; she is your foe, and she must be vanquished.
(Oh, and then you have to tour with her eleven months out of the
year on the competition circuit. No big.)

This intensely individual competition might explain why
tennis pros aren't exactly known for their cozy interpersonal relationships. Instead, you hear how Roger Federer and Rafael Nadal

are wicked rivals. How Maria Sharapova isn't out there to make friends. How Steffi Graf and Monica Seles never spoke a word to each other. Steffi told *Tennis* magazine that this hypercompetitiveness and the antisociability it breeds were particularly prevalent on the women's circuit and that "the rivalry among women players is overwhelming." This makes sense, considering that girls are often raised under the patriarchal assumption that in any situation, there's room for only one woman. We're constantly taught to be competing for jobs, partners, possessions, praise. Add to the mix the stereotype that competitiveness is unladylike, and you can understand where the underhanded "cattiness" business comes from.

In the 2010 book *Tennis and Philosophy*, scholars David Baggett and Neil Delaney Jr. theorize that there have been some tennis relationships that Aristotle would've called "friendships of pleasure" ("I enjoy playing tennis with this person, but it's just about the sport—the person is interchangeable") and "friendships of usefulness" ("I enjoy playing tennis with this person because I get to improve my game"). But rare is the most meaningful type, "friendships of virtue," the ones in which two people genuinely care for each other on such a deep level that a win for either feels like a win for both. A friendship in which mutual respect transcends jealousy and each gal truly wants the best for the other, even if that sometimes means not getting the top prize. A friendship in which winning isn't the only thing that matters.

And that's what makes those rare friendships so amazing. Chris Evert and Martina Navratilova have perhaps the most canonical tennis friendship, with Serena Williams and Caroline

Wozniacki also palling around even under intense competition. And then there's Madison Keys and Sloane Stephens, besties who at ages 24 and 22 faced each other at the final match of the 2017 US Open.

It was an intense match-up in more ways than one, but it was also fitting that the two women ended up in the same place at the same time—their careers have followed a remarkably similar path. Both grew up and trained in Florida and Southern California; both dealt with the pressure and expectations of being labeled "prodigies"; both are women of color thriving in a field that has been less than welcoming. They made their names in tennis as semifinalists in the Australian Open—Sloane in 2013, after beating Serena Williams in the quarterfinals, and Madison in 2015. And they've been friends since they were junior pros, playing together in tournaments and on Fed Cup teams.

Their friendship solidified early in the 2017 season, when each found herself injured and benched—Madison was recovering from two wrist surgeries, and Sloane had been off her feet for ten months following foot surgery. During that year's Australian Open, they were stuck at home convalescing. "I think we both just texted each other and said: 'This really sucks,'" recalled Madison at a 2017 press conference. "From then on, I have always been talking to her and texting her, keeping in touch. I think we have really helped each other. I think we have definitely known what each other was going through throughout the year." Each helped the other gain perspective during their time off the court, realizing they appreciated what they do—as well as each other. "Whenever we are around, we try to go to dinner . . . and hang out," Madison said at the same press conference. "More than that, she's always someone who I know is always there watching. She'll text me no matter what. We are always keeping tabs on each other and rooting for each other."

These two buds knew that very sentiment would be tested upon hearing they'd be facing off in the final of the US Open. The match-up was unexpected; just six weeks before the tournament, Sloane was ranked outside the top 950 players in the world, making her only the third woman in the history of tennis ranked below the top fifty to make the final. "Getting to play my friend," Madison said at a press conference, "it's just an amazing opportunity. I'm going to go out there and do my absolute best." Sloane immediately agreed: "I love her to death. It's obviously going to be tough. It's not easy playing a friend."

In September, the two buds walked onto the Arthur Ashe Stadium courts for this dramatic match, knowing that one would leave with her first-ever Grand Slam win. Not only was this the first time two American women would be hitting in the final since the Venus vs. Serena showdown in 2002, but it was also the first time that three of the tournament's four semifinalists were Black women. Sloane (whose mother, Sybil Smith, was the first Black woman to be named a First Team All-American athlete in Division I history, in 1988) told the *Guardian* there wasn't "any word to describe it other than 'amazing' for me and Maddie and obviously, Venus." That it also happened to be the sixtieth anniversary of Althea Gibson's US Nationals win—the first victory by a Black woman in the tournament that became the US Open—made the match even more historic. "We are following in her footsteps," said Sloane. "She's been here. She's represented the game so well as an African American woman. Maddie and I are here to join her and represent just as well as Venus has in the past, and [are] honored to be here."

The stakes were high, but the match didn't end up even remotely close: Sloane demolished a nerve-wracked Madison 6–3, 6–0. Yet the landslide victory wasn't the biggest story to come out of the match. The most memorable part for the press, the spectators, and the world was when Sloane leapt to the net to take her friend into her arms. The embrace lasted only about twenty seconds, but it felt, on camera and to the 23,000 fans in the stands, like an eternity: Sloane letting Madison cry into her shoulder, consoling her best bud over the loss of what was the biggest victory of her life. In Madison's ear, Sloane whispered that she wished the match could have been a draw. Because the loser isn't permitted to leave the court before the trophy ceremony, Sloane sat with Madison to pass the time, instead of remaining on the opposite side of the court, as is typical. As the minutes ticked by and Sloane kept up a conversation, Madison's expression changed from tears to a smile and eventually, even, to laughter.

"Sloane is truly one of my favorite people, and to get to play her was really special," Madison said at the post-match press conference. "We have known each other for so long and we have been through so much that we wanted to share that moment with each other. To be able to share my first Slam experience with a really close friend when it's also her first Slam is a really special moment. There's no one else in the world that would have meant as much as it did." Sloane agreed wholeheartedly: "Maddie is one of my bestest friends on tour, if not my best friend on tour, and to play her here—honestly, I wouldn't have wanted to play anyone else—but for us both to be here is such a special moment." When reporters asked about their post-game embrace, Sloane was quick to compliment her friend yet again. "I think that if it was the other way around, she would do the same for me, and I'm going to support her no matter what," she said. "I know she's going to support me no matter what, so to stand up here today with her is incredible—and that's what real friendship is."

The two joked that they would be going out that night for celebratory drinks—on Sloane. Madison praised Sloane's talent and her ability to bounce back after injury. When Sloane was presented with the massive $3.7 million check, she grabbed Madison's arm, pretending to faint. Madison joked, "I'll hold it for her!"

If their friendship has a common value, it's sportsmanship. The previous year, after playing a different opponent, Sloane told the *Washington Post* how much she appreciated "when other people gracefully take their loss." You have to imagine that one year later, on the court of the US Open, Madison's graceful acceptance of her loss would have done nothing but increase their mutual love and respect. Like Chris and Martina or Serena and Caroline before them, that attitude displays a rock-solid level of friendship to which we can all aspire. ✦

CHAPTER 2

POLITICAL & ACTIVIST SQUADS

S tanding up for what you believe in is no
easy task, especially if the world tells you
that you would do better to be seen rather than
heard. The good news is that it's a heck of a lot
easier to stand up to the Man when the Gals
have got your back. Let's take a look at some of
history's most tough-as-nails squads and be inspired by the actions they took to improve their
lives and the lives of all the women they knew.

Trưng Trắc and Trưng Nhị

THE VIETNAMESE SISTERS
WHO LED AN UPRISING

CIRCA 20 CE–43 CE

It sounds like the stuff of epic legends (or at least a badass fantasy novel): Two sisters riding into battle on elephants, swords drawn. Two sisters stopping a man-eating tiger in its tracks with a deadly spear to the heart. Two sisters unleashing their ruthlessly effective combat skills to beat back oppression and imperialism. But it's no myth. It's the Trưng sisters.

Like anything that happened roughly two thousand years ago, the exact details of the Trưng sisters' lives are not only few and far between, they're also reported through the lens of Men with Agendas. Nevertheless, some things we know for sure. Shortly before 200 BCE, China started to gear up for some imperial conquests (i.e., looking at neighboring nations and thinking,

"Yeah, I could for sure own that."). By 208 BCE, the Qin dynasty general Zhao Tuo had reached what the Chinese considered the edge of "civilization," an area encompassing southern China and northern Vietnam that was settled mostly by a group of indigenous peoples whom the Chinese called the Yue. After conquering and annexing a bunch of territory, Zhao Tuo declared himself king of Nanyue. (The term Nanyue means, essentially, Southern Yue and is pronounced "nam vee-et" in modern Vietnamese). For the better part of a century his kingdom coexisted—sometimes peacefully, sometimes not—as a sort of independent tributary of imperial China. For the most part, the Yue were left to their own devices; even after the Han dynasty conquered Nanyue in 111 BCE, seizing control back from Zhao Tuo, the northern Vietnamese people were subject to only nominal taxation and were largely able to maintain their traditional customs, culture, and rulership without imperial interference. For a while.

Around the turn of the first millennium, the situation got way less chill for those near China's borders. The emperor of Han China had set his sights on the Red River Delta, an area of today's northern Vietnam inhabited by the Lạc Việt, a group of Yue tribes that was part of the independent Âu Lạc state until it was annexed into Nanyue by Zhao Tuo around 179 BCE. The region was a killer supply point, and the Han wanted to "civilize" it. So they sent officials down to Nanyue to seize land and convert it into Chinese farms to be tended by Chinese peasants. This led to the establishment of local Chinese schools, art, language, music, architecture, and religion—all of which supplanted the cultural institutions that made the Yue people, well, their own people.

To compound all that bad, the Han dynasty started enforcing laws and imposing taxes upon the Nanyue's hereditary district chiefs, known as the Lac lords, probably on items like crafted goods, tropical products (like oranges), salt, and perhaps even fishing in local rivers. (Of course, in lieu of paying these taxes, you could work for free for your new Chinese lord.) Add to that the political unrest back in China (the Han dynasty was interrupted when military dictator Wang Mang seized the throne from 9 CE to 23 CE) that saw refugees fleeing south in droves. Overall, the Yue people found themselves increasingly at risk of complete Sinicization, or total integration into Chinese culture. Needless to say, the Lac lords and their people were not thrilled with this forcible cultural overhaul—and it was into this environment that the Trưng sisters were born, around 20 CE.

Unlike most women in this era, Trắc and her younger sister Nhị didn't experience many disadvantages because of their gender. One of the myriad interesting things about ancient Viet society is that there wasn't as much discrimination against women as existed among their northern Confucian cousins (or, like, much of the rest of the world). Viet society was likely matriarchal or matrilineal until about the seventh century BCE, at which point bilateral kinship became the norm, which meant that men and women enjoyed equal treatment in matters of inheritance and descendance. This type of equality might have been born out of the Vietnamese peoples' creation myth, which goes something like this: Âu Cơ, the fairy bird mother, loved the dragon king's son Lac Long Quân, and together they had one hundred sons, who became the first people of Vietnam. But when Âu Cơ and Lac Long Quân realized they were fundamentally different people, they parted on good terms, each taking fifty sons (v. conscious uncoupling, if you ask me). This matriarchal–patriarchal sentiment is reflected in Vietnamese laws dating from most of the common era: daughters could inherit property the same way sons could (although probably *less* property), break an engagement or initiate divorce under circumstances more lenient than those for men, perform ancestor worship, decline a marriage proposal, and avoid enslavement.

So, as daughters of the well-liked Lac lord of the northern Mê Linh district, the Trưng sisters were treated as proper heirs to his title, even sharing a last name with the first rulers of Vietnam (though they likely were not related). Oral tradition suggests that Trắc and Nhị were raised with an intense dislike of the Han; although no written evidence confirms this, it seems believable, given what we know of the deliberate attempt by the Chinese to seize Yue lands and wipe out the indigenous culture to which the Trưngs belonged. As the youngest in a long line of hereditary military rulers, Trắc and Nhị likely would have been educated together on the old ways of their people, including how to be megabadasses on the battlefield (let's just say "How to Train your War Elephant" was likely part of the curriculum).

Though Nhị probably never married, Trắc, who is described in Chinese records as "of brave and fearless disposition," met and fell in love with Thi Sách, the son of the Lac lord of Chu-Điện, a village not far from the sisters' home district. Sách, "of fierce temperament," according to his enemies, shared Trắc's values, and once married the couple fought hard against Han oppression—

so hard that Sū Dìng, the local Chinese prefect, went out of his way to impose laws on Sách that made it nearly impossible for Trắc and her husband to effectively rule their people.

This round of restrictions was the last straw for the Trưng sisters. Infuriated at the way their people were being disrespected, and about the particularly harsh laws the Han had imposed on their family, the gals were like, "You know what? You guys can go now." In 40 CE, they ordered the Lac lords to mobilize their forces (and maybe their elephants) and beat back Sū Dìng and his compatriots nearly five hundred miles north, to Guangzhou. Though smaller disputes had broken out before, the Trưng sisters' rebellion was the first successful major uprising against the Chinese in Vietnamese history. They killed it. Literally.

Once Trắc and Nhị had cleared out the invaders, they wasted no time regaining control of their lands, and then some. Trắc installed herself in Mê Linh as queen, with Nhị likely at her side as co-queen. By embracing and encouraging the area's indigenous culture, religion, art, and language—oh, and abolishing all those preposterous taxes—the Trưngs were able to attract sixty-five other coastal tribes and settlements to get on board with their "we're an independent nation and the Chinese are *out of here*" plan. Not bad, considering they were only in their twenties at the time. (And their epicness didn't end there: popular folklore includes a wicked story about how the sisters hunted a man-eating tiger in public, with Nhị launching a spear into its heart after it threw Trắc to the ground, then skinning it and carving their dedication to independence into its hide.) According to oral tradition and temple records, when they had assembled their army no fewer than thirty-six of the sisters' high-ranking generals were women, including their own mother.

Of course, the Han emperor was not stoked about these developments. By the next year, he had commanded 56-year-old general Ma (a traditional Mandarin word meaning "horse") Yüan, a practiced rebellion-crusher known as "the general who calms the waves," to head to the Red River Delta and reassert Chinese control. It took him and his twenty thousand men a while, but early in 43 CE, they arrived at the Trưngs' lands and trounced the sisters' army. Many of the indigenous fighters were killed or captured, but a significant number simply surrendered—perhaps because the encroaching influence of Confucian patriarchy had led them to lose faith in their women leaders, or possibly because the Chinese just flat-out brought more soldiers (or both).

Sadly, the sisters did not survive. How they died depends on whose account you believe: the Chinese version says that their troops captured the Trưngs and sent their heads back to the Han court, whereas the Vietnamese will tell you that the sisters drowned themselves in a river to avoid capture. In any case, afterward Ma Yüan reannexed the Red River Delta to China and melted down the Yue peoples' bronze drums—which were traditionally played while riding into battle and symbolized the power of their chiefs—recasting them into a bronze horse. Despite the sisters' incredible efforts, the cultural and political invasion of their homeland by the Chinese was viciously thorough.

Despite their eventual defeat, Trắc and Nhị proudly ruled for three years, embracing what made the Yue people unique and interesting and wonderful all on their own. (Some scholars today even believe that, without the Trưng sisters as a guiding light, the Vietnamese would not have continued to resist Sinicization as forcefully as they did.) In the two millennia that followed this rad reign of sister power, their story has been told and retold at length, which means a lot of dude historians have shaped it to mean what they want it to mean, depending on where and when they're writing from. In 1272—a time when Vietnamese society was heavily patriarchal—the historian Le Van Huu wrote that during the Trưng rebellion "the men of our land bowed their heads, folded their arms, and served the northerners; how shameful this is in comparison with the two Trưng sisters, who were women! Ah, it is enough to make one want to die!" Way to use the Trưng sisters as a symbol of dishonor instead of pride, my guy.

This theme of shaming men for "letting" women do the fighting appears later, in a poem from the fifteenth century whose author has not been recorded or translated in the English scholarship, and again in another unattributed poem from the seventeenth century: "It was not even a man, But a mere girl who wielded the skill of a hero!" Basically, the further you get from 43 CE, the more not-at-all-positive commentary you hear about the Trưng sisters' gender. An oft-repeated narrative insists that Sách was murdered by Sū Dìng, painting Trắc as an emotional and sentimental girl who was *forced* to sacrifice her femininity to fight, motivated largely by personal revenge. (Because obviously a woman couldn't be a queen if her husband was still alive, what nonsense!) Other versions exaggerate Trắc's sense of patriotic duty, transforming her into a nationalist symbol rather than portraying her as an actual human woman. These tales often justified such portrayals with a (made-up) quote in which Trắc declares: "First, I will avenge my country / Second, I will restore the Hung royal lineage, / Third, I will avenge the death of my husband, / Lastly, I vow that these goals will be accomplished."

Beyond dragging their military abilities or motivations for rebellion through the mud, some writers gave creepy details about the sisters' physical appearance (never mind that we don't even know what they looked like). Poets waxed on about their beauty ("snow-white shoulders, fragrant breath, skin of ivory," and so on) while condemning those very features as weak ("her followers, seeing that she was a woman, feared she could not stand up to the enemy and consequently dispersed"). Then there's the standard misogynistic takedowns, like one guy who blames defeat on the sisters just not doing as they were told. Still other accounts claim that the sisters lost the war because Chinese men would take out their man-bits on the battlefield, which shocked the women into standing still until their throats were cut. (Because on a battle-field littered with dead bodies, *that* is what would've freaked them out? Please.)

All of this sexist speculation is just that: speculation. We will never know everything about these Vietnamese patriots, but we do know that they were fiercely devoted to and protective of their culture and their people. They were sisters and daughters with friends and family and lovers, all of whom they had to watch get treated poorly by people they regarded as invaders. And though it might be appalling to those old-timey scholars, more accurate speculation suggests that the Trưng sisters were vengeful widows and patriotic heroes and angry and sad and righteous and kickass all at the same time. Because women are people, and people are complicated. Go figure.

The good news is that, unlike so many forgotten heroines in history, Trắc and Nhị sprouted their very own long-lasting spirit cult in Vietnam. As far back as the 1400s, prayers to the sisters for rain were said to have "never gone unanswered"; a twelfth-century king reportedly appealed to the Trưngs to end a drought and was rewarded not only with much-needed showers but also a dream of "two pretty-faced women with willowy eyebrows wearing green robes over red garments with red crowns and sashes, astride iron horses, passing by with the rain." (They were already on top of that full brow trend! What *can't* the Trưngs do?) Even today, the story of how the brave Trưng sisters stood up to the Chinese invaders occupies a place in Vietnamese cultural consciousness. Temples, districts, streets, and schools across the country are dedicated to them, and the relatively greater autonomy of women citizens throughout history that they exemplified is a point of pride for Vietnamese cultural historians. The annual festival known as Hai Ba Trưng (The Two Ladies Trưng), celebrated from the third to sixth days of the second lunar month, is believed to coincide with the Trưngs' death and honors the women and their sacrifice. (That it happens just a few days before International Women's Day is an awesome coincidence.)

So the next time you start to wonder about what women have done to fight cultural assimilation (like, tomorrow, say), just remember Trắc and Nhị Trưng, the literally ride-or-die sister duo who became the coolest co-queens of Vietnam. ✦

Manon Roland and Sophie Grandchamp

THE ARISTOCRATIC BEST FRIENDS WITH A FRONT-ROW SEAT TO THE FRENCH REVOLUTION

1754–1793

Bloodshed. Baguettes. Bouffant hairdos stuffed with birds and butterflies. The French Revolution is the perfect backdrop for angst—but what about fantastic female friendship? Well, don't you worry, *mes amies*: it had *beaucoup* of that too, thanks to *les filles fantastiques* Manon Roland and Sophie Grandchamp.

Depending on how well-versed you are in *Hamilton* (get it? Versed? That's a little musical humor, there), you may not know much about the French Revolution. Suffice it to say that its nuts and bolts are standard-issue political uprising: in the late 1700s, France was still a monarchy run by King Louis XVI, whose wasteful spending and apathy toward his citizens, especially the poor ones, was contributing to massive social and financial inequality. Meanwhile, the French people were looking at England, with its fancy constitution, and America, which was fighting hard for a little thing called democracy, and thinking, *Mm, that looks pretty good right about now.* The anti-royalty revolutionaries, who called themselves Jacobins, soon numbered in the hundreds of thousands. The Jacobins, in turn, were largely made up of two groups: the Girondists, who originally supported the establishment of a constitutional monarchy with the king as a figurehead (like Canada), and *La Montagne*, or the Mountain, super-radicals very much in favor of effectively just murdering everyone who disagreed with them, the king included. Cue infighting amongst the nobility and Jacobins, outfighting between the upper and lower classes, street-dance fighting away from Javert, guillotines, and so on.

It was in 1754, amidst these early rumblings of revolution, that Marie-Jeanne Phlippon (better known to her buds as Manon) was born to an aristocratic French family. Manon was a voracious reader, particularly fascinated by philosophy and religion. When she was a young woman, her family sent her to a convent to further her education, an experience she welcomed, especially after having to rebuff the advances of teenage boys beginning when she was around ten years old. (Solidarity, sister.) While at the convent, Manon, who tended throughout her life to judge people quickly and with finality, struck up what would be the first of two incredibly intense female friendships, this one with her schoolmate Sophie Cannet. Though they parted at a young age, Manon and Sophie (well, mostly Manon) wrote constantly, and for the rest of their lives, about literally everything. Sometimes Manon's letters dove deep into her daily life or what she found most interesting about Plutarch's heroes; sometimes they would be long train-of-thought strings of nonsense words that merely gave an impression of her current mood. (In an 1893 profile of Manon's life, the writer Ida M. Tarbell called these missives "ardent love letters," noting that Manon would "suffer tortures" when Sophie's letters were late; she even started devising ways to improve the postal service to hasten their correspondence. Just gals bein' pals? Make of that what you will.)

As tends to happen, the more she read, the more Manon came to view the world through a particular lens. In this case, after reading Rousseau and Plutarch, she started to dream about a French republic, a new kind of government founded on justice and virtue and equality and liberty and other noble-sounding Enlightenment stuff. In 1780, after traveling around Europe, the 26-year-old Manon met and married 46-year-old Jean-Marie Roland, a manufacturing inspector. (Yes, her name was Marie-Jeanne and his was Jean-Marie. They're French, it happens.) The couple moved to Villefranche, a small town outside Lyon, in southeastern France. There, while raising their only daughter, Eudora, Manon became politically active, ghostwriting liberal articles for her husband that appeared in revolutionary papers and pamphlets. These efforts gained the couple entry into revolutionary, anti-monarchy, Jacobin (and particularly Girondist) circles in Paris when they visited in February 1791.

Mere days before Manon's trip back to Villefranche, a Jacobin and botanist friend named Louis-Augustin Bosc d'Antic (known by his Bono-like nickname, Bosc) was dead-set that Manon meet one Sophie Grandchamp, an educated Parisian and extremely well-liked teacher. Sophie provided free courses to girls in astronomy, grammar, and literature and would later translate works by Aphra Behn and Helen Maria Williams. Upon introducing the two thirtysomething women, Bosc simply said: "Here is an Athenian, whom I present to a Spartan."

Sophie never forgot her first impression of Manon (already renowned among the Jacobins for her writing as well as her taste in powerful friends), clothed in what Sophie described as an "Amazonian dress" with hair tied back in a coachman's style, framing "gentle and penetrating eyes." She was so taken by Manon's "remarkable" intelligence and charm that she tried twice (both times unsuccessfully) to visit the busy woman at home. Imagine her shock when, a few days later, Manon flew into her rooms, running to give her a hug and a kiss and declaring that "our souls are *en rapport*; we must love each other." (Manon had a thing for Sophies, apparently.) Devastated to leave for Villefranche so soon after meeting Sophie, Manon insisted her new friend join her—which Manon managed by kicking her maid out of the carriage. (Remember equality, Manon? Ah, well.)

Of the five-day journey to the countryside in September 1791, Sophie wrote that she and Manon talked constantly and late into the night about the entirety of their lives, with Manon sharing secrets about her relationship with Jean-Marie, her way of life, and her innermost feelings. Sophie called these hours *délicieuses*—"delightful" or "delicious," depending on your read—and, before she knew it, she wrote, "*je m'occupais déjà des moyens de la rendre plus heureuse; mon bonheur commençait à dépendre du sien*" (I was already occupying myself with ways to make her happier; my happiness began to depend on hers).

Though the trip was tiresome, with the women rising at odd hours to catch coaches and boats, they barely noticed. In her 1917 biography of Manon, British author Una Pope-Hennessy wrote that Manon found her trip with Sophie "so very gay and so deeply interested in their never-ending conversation, that discomforts did not really matter." Once in Villefranche, Sophie found profound joy and solitude with "*la plus séduisante des femmes*" (the most seductive of women); in her journals, as translated by Una, she wrote: "it was in this rustic place, in this profound solitude, that I realized the value of intercourse with this most attractive of women." Aren't gal pals just the best?

After arriving in Villefranche, Sophie stayed with Manon for three weeks before Jean-Marie showed up and crashed their party. The ladies escaped to sightsee in Lyon for a bit, but when they returned, Jean-Marie killed the mood again by asking Sophie to make notes on a two-hundred-plus-page section of his *Dictionnaire des manufactures*, part of an expanded *Encyclopédie*, originally edited by Denis Diderot. Learning from Manon that Jean-Marie took criticism poorly (Manon was basically like, you can say nothing and he'll be mad that you're dumb, or break it to him gently and he'll ... still be mad, actually), Sophie left a few brief notes and fled back to Paris around the end of October. Though she was distraught about the possibility of never again seeing her best friend, she simply could not deal with Jean-Marie. Manon cried for days, fearing they'd never be reunited.

Luckily, that was not to be. Within a few weeks, when Jean-Marie's job was abolished and he found himself unemployed (along with all the other inspectors), Manon convinced him to move to Paris full-time and get involved in the revolution. When the couple arrived on December 15, 1791, Sophie found and furnished an apartment for her friend (and her friend's husband, I guess) near her own home. She had waited in agony to be reunited with Manon, writing, "*je calculais le jour, l'heure où je la presserais contre mon coeur*" (I calculated the day, the hour when I could press her against my heart), and visited Manon and Jean-Marie on the night of their arrival. Once there, Sophie again felt spurned by Jean-Marie; she stormed home and immediately wrote him an angry letter about how he'd disrespected her (she made a copy for herself so she could read it with satisfaction later). The instant she sent the letter off with her maid, Sophie heard a knock on her door—it was Jean-Marie, there to beg her forgiveness. From then on, Sophie, Manon, and Jean-Marie kept close company during the rest of their time in Paris.

The Rolands quickly became active in the revolutionary scene—just as Manon had wanted. The most politically active woman in their social circles, Manon led a salon (or what she called "the little committee") out of her home, which was attended by all the most important men of the revolution, such as Maximilien Robespierre, François Buzot, Jérôme Pétion, and Jacques Pierre Brissot. Though Manon was always careful to play the role of silent hostess, pretty much everyone knew she was the brains of the operation; many modern scholars have noted that she was more politically savvy than all the male activists who gathered in her house combined. She used her charm to calm arguments and facilitate discussions, all while taking notes to better form her opinions on the direction of the future French government. "I never lost a word of what was said," Manon recalled, "and it happened sometimes that I had to bite my tongue to keep from saying what I thought." She loved pretending to be the perfect domestic while secretly running the show, and she "particularly enjoy[ed] listening to old men who imagine that every word they say is a revelation to the listener and who think that all I am capable of is stitching a shirt and adding up figures." Meanwhile, Jean-Marie finally learned to take constructive criticism, so Sophie acted as his secretary, working for him in the mornings before spending the afternoons with her best bud.

As the months passed and Manon grew impatient for change (specifically the enfranchisement of women and a democratic revolution), she fell into a deep depression, tiring of living mostly in poverty and obscurity, which Sophie attributed to the "secret ambition that she nourished." Basically, Manon was a little bit bored and a little bit jealous of her more politically successful friends—until March 22, 1792, that is, when Jean-Marie was offered the position of Minister of the Interior. The Girondist political faction (the less radical and more philosophical branch of the Jacobins), to which the Rolands adhered, had recently come into legislative power by convincing the king to fill his ministry with their numbers. They were working to convince him to declare war on Austria, which they hoped would dissuade foreign powers from helping Louis quash the revolutionaries and, perhaps, spread the revolution throughout Europe. The king, for his part, figured that rallying against a common enemy might bolster patriotism (and get everyone off his back a little).

Naturally, such an offer required a consult from a close friend, so Manon and Jean-Marie invited Sophie over to discuss the job. Upon arriving the next morning, Sophie was shocked to see the change that had come over the place. "My friend, who had been on the point of death that morning," Sophie remembered, "had recovered her freshness and graces; she was surrounded by a numerous circle of people who loaded her with praises." The Rolands accepted the position, asking Sophie, who was familiar with the court and nobility since birth, to act as a kind of mistress of ceremonies, receiving the minister's visitors and analyzing their behavior, as well as collecting and reporting on articles written about him. During their time in power, Manon and Sophie's relationship suffered some ups and downs, often because of Manon's all-consuming ambitions, but they were two people with emotions in the midst of the French Revolution. I sometimes get into fights with my BFF when I'm stressed over, like, what to watch on Netflix. Manon and Sophie were under an exponential amount of stress. So their occasional tiffs? Understandable.

Alas, as the revolution continued, the tide began to turn against the moderate Girondists. One of the most influential revolutionaries and a Mountaineer, Maximilien Robespierre, even accused Jean-Marie and the Girondists of being run by a "female triumvirate" who duped and corrupted their husbands into doing their bidding while living as extravagantly as King Louis XV's notorious mistress, Madame de Pompadour. In response to a letter written by Manon (it was signed "Jean-Marie," but we

all know who really wrote it) demanding that the king continue to support the Girondists, Jean-Marie lost his ministerial job.
The rest of their group was swiftly kicked out of their official positions too. The Mountaineers were tired of the Girdonists and
their perceived "royalist sympathies." They wanted the king executed—and any and all of his supporters, too. By spring 1793,
with the Mountain revvin' up for the Reign of Terror (and, like,
the zillion murders that would entail), Manon and the other Girondists had been arrested for treason.

Manon spent her remaining days in two French prisons,
where she was visited by several of her women friends but mostly
(of course) by Sophie, who came by almost daily. In jail, Manon
began to write her memoirs, which she imagined would "amuse
people very much one of these days," and gave the pages to Sophie,
who smuggled them out and hid them in a beam above a church
door, where (hopefully) no one would think to look during a government raid. Sophie also convinced the jailers to provide Manon
with a piano, books, and drawing materials. Another friend
helped improve conditions for Manon: During Jean-Marie's days
of political influence, Sophie recommended her friend Grandpré
(possibly the Parisian lawyer Pierre-Claude Lemoyne de Grandpré, with whom she may have been living by 1792 and may have
had a child) for the job of prison inspector, and Manon advocated for his appointment. Thanks to him, Sophie was able to visit
the imprisoned Manon much more frequently and for much longer periods than was typically allowed.

Still, prison life was not the best. After a desperate Manon
tried to starve herself to death, Sophie visited her in the infirmary,

where they talked about the weather, Jean-Marie, and Manon's doctor. At another point, they likely overheard from Manon's cell the committee in charge of the massacres eating dinner in the adjacent room and gleefully discussing Manon's future execution. When Sophie visited on October 29, 1793, to tell Manon that the rest of the Girondists had been executed, Manon wept—but only for her country. As she told her friend, "My own fate is fixed; there is no more uncertainty. I shall join them in a little while, and show myself worthy of following them." Manon had given up on suicide, knowing that the guillotine was inevitable.

Understandably distraught by the thought of her impending death at the hands of what would surely be an angry mob, Manon begged Sophie to return the next day, despite the now very-imminent threat of death for anyone with even a whiff of "royalist" about them; Sophie stayed up the whole night coming up with a convincing disguise. When she returned, Manon asked: "Would you have the courage to be there at my last moments, in order that you can give an authentic testimony of how they were?" Sophie agreed; the following day, she'd stand on the first step of the Pont Neuf bridge with a view of Manon's walk to the guillotine, disguised exactly as she was now so that Manon could find her, even from afar. Manon was determined not to be shamed by the crowd in her last moments, as were many women and so-called traitors; she wanted Sophie to tell the world that she was brave and confident and virtuous. The two women talked for three more hours, though Sophie could never quite remember about what. They didn't cry. With one last hug, Manon sent Sophie away before she could be caught.

The next day, Sophie walked to the bridge, trying to convince herself that Plutarch would want her to *envy* those about to die (which, no offense to Plutarch, is not a comforting thought). Though she recognized a ton of people in the crowd and was terrified of being spotted, Sophie stood where she said she would. When Manon stepped into the light, Sophie saw her smiling, looking fresh, even helping to calm the condemned person next to her. Their eyes met across the distance, and Sophie saw in Manon's face "the satisfaction that she felt to see me at this last unforgettable rendezvous; as she came level with me, a movement of her eyes, accompanied by a smile, told me she was glad to have her wish fulfilled." Once Manon was out of sight, Sophie fled home. Waiting for her there were the rest of Manon's Jacobin friends, who stayed together while Manon lost her head.

Both Manon's *Mémoires* and Sophie's *Souvenirs* discuss at length the depth of these women's connection and love for each other. Manon valued Sophie until the end, and Sophie never forgot her friend (though she later wished she had convinced Jean-Marie not to take the Ministry position and to flee to the countryside instead). Together, they managed not only to write, discuss, and direct some of the most revolutionary political thoughts of their day, but they also carved out a little piece of paradise in a hugely unstable (and often deadly) period of Western political history. Sophie and Manon forced a country toward democracy, and their friendship managed to survive the turmoil—and even, in the end, the guillotine. For them, "friends 'til the end" wasn't just a saying. It was a promise. ✦

The Patriotic Women's League of Iran

*THE PERSIAN WOMEN WHO FOUGHT
FOR EQUAL RIGHTS*

ACTIVE 1922–1933

"You can kill me as soon as you like, but you cannot stop the emancipation of women." So said Táhirih, a Persian woman condemned to death in 1852. A poet and scholar, Táhirih was notable not only because she subscribed to the minority Bayání faith, but also because she unveiled herself in public in 1848—an unthinkable act at the time. Both were crimes punishable by death. Though Táhirih perished in the name of freedom, her proclamation came true sixty years later, when the Patriotic Women's League of Iran arrived on the scene and demanded equal treatment for women.

At the turn of the twentieth century, most of Iran's current cultural practices vis-à-vis women dated back to the 1500s, when the Safavid dynasty took control of the country and (largely to affirm their power) declared Shiism, a branch of Islam, the national religion. The financially independent *ulama*, or Shia clergy, strongly influenced not only the country's political, legal, and educational systems but citizens' social lives as well. The *ulama* established a patriarchy that allowed men to engage in polygamy and subjected women to mandatory wearing of headscarves, confinement to the home, and young, blind, and temporary marriages. (Note that patriarchy was widespread in late medieval Europe and Biblical language was used to justify male control of women. So, you know, #YesAllMen.) The practice of sequestering women continued virtually unchallenged in Iran until around the late 1800s—which is not to say that women liked it. (Imagine being confined to not just your house, but the innermost rooms, so that no passersby could even accidentally glimpse you in a freak window-glancing accident. You probably wouldn't like that, either.) But the winds of change had been stirring for a long time: the Qajar dynasty, which took control in 1785, had backed themselves into a corner financially. Between their extravagant lifestyle, a debilitating reliance on taxed imported goods, and military defeats at the hands of the Russian Empire in 1828 and the British Empire in 1857, the Qajars were forced to accept foreign money to start paying off debts. And with foreign money came foreign influence, for better or worse. As the twentieth century approached, Iranian society increasingly pressured the monarchy both to embrace modernization and secularization and to shake off royal corruption and foreign imperialist control. The intense desire of the Iranian people to make their country a democratized and parliamentary nation took hold, leading to the Constitutional Revolution in 1906, which was followed by about a decade of turbulence.

Of course, when I say "the Iranian people" I mean mostly "Iranian men"; women weren't legally allowed to leave the house, spend their own money, participate in religious practices without permission, or refuse to have sex with their husbands, let alone engage in political debate. When these men drafted the constitution in 1906, they didn't give women the right to vote, or . . . well, any rights, actually. Under this new system, women were considered subjects of their fathers and husbands, and they were included in the same legal category as the "fraudulent, bankrupt, beggars, and all those who earn their living in a disreputable way." The *ulama*, who still controlled schools and laws, thought that women's emancipation was all about moral corruption and easy sex and the loss of "male honor." A representative of the highest religious authority said that "God has not given [women] the capacity for taking part in politics and electing the representation of this nation" and that the "weaker sex" did not have "the same power of judgment" as men. (Lest anyone assume that this sexism was unique to Iran, recall that Charles Darwin wrote in 1896's *The Descent of Man* that men were inarguably superior because of their "higher eminence" in anything "requiring deep thought, reason, or imagination, or merely the use of the senses and hands." Also remember that preeminent nineteenth-century evolutionist Joseph LeConte opposed suffrage for women because their lack of "*formal* reason" meant they were biologically incapable of making informed decisions. Just sayin'.)

But different perspectives started to take hold around the country, one of which was "maybe literally one-half of the population responsible for raising our children should somehow be active participants in our new nation." Iranian women had historically not been permitted to organize into political associations, thanks to super-harsh punishments (remember Táhirih?). In 1906, however, women began protesting in the streets, especially in the capital of Tehran. Women also hid revolutionary activists in their homes, organized strikes, spread news, and even carried guns under their veils. (Now *that* is the Bourne movie I am *waiting* for.) And these actions weren't exclusively focused on what we might call women's issues. These activists supported the fight for Iran's nationhood, constitutionalism, and, especially, better education for all future citizens. As the National Ladies Society (founded in 1910 as the Women's Society) wrote in response to a letter questioning why they were fighting for expanded rights, the women of Iran were "not content with [their] status and position" and "consider[ed] the position of European women favorable because they possess[ed] skills, but not for any other reasons." They firmly believed that the establishment of a constitution and parliament would also mean the legal establishment of a code of equality. After all, everyone was fighting for the same thing: improved status for all Iranian people, regardless of gender. Right?

Not exactly. The sentiment was there, but the political progress, not so much. In 1911, Vakil al-Ru'aya, parliamentary deputy and ally to the cause, tried to raise the issue, boldly declaring that women "possessed souls and rights, and should possess votes." As he spoke, the *Times* of London reported, "the House shivered," and after listening in "dead silence" to Vakil's speech, the jurist in charge of interpreting Islamic law said he'd "never in a life of misfortune had his ears assailed by such an impious utterance." He then "denied to women either souls or rights, and declared that such doctrine would mean the downfall of Islam." The Iranian president asked transcribers to strike Vakil's entire speech from the official record.

By no means was such stonewalling good for the cause, although it *did* provide the impetus for a lot of understandably angry Iranian women to dedicate themselves even more intensely to organizing, publishing, and fighting for their own, specific rights. A new twentieth-century generation of writers and activists was bolstered in part by nineteenth-century gals like Taj al-Saltaneh, the harem-raised daughter of a Qajar shah whose memoirs revealed her frustrations with the limitations of her life, and Bibi Khanum Astarabadi, who, in her mid-thirties, wrote a response to a widely distributed anonymous pamphlet titled *Ta'dib al-Nesvan* (How to Discipline Women), which was exactly what you think it is. Her response, *Ma'ayib al-Rijal* (Vices of Men), was composed in the style of contemporary male advice texts, except that it laid out all the ways in which men are problematic, pointing out that all of Iran's issues were inherently the fault of men because women had no say. It advised men to "give up trying to discipline women and try to discipline and educate themselves." (Can I get a hell yeah?) With writers like Bibi and Taj as inspirations, women of the early 1900s formed their first official *anjumans* (political associations)—the most active of which was

Jam'iyat-e nesvan, the Patriotic Women's League (PWL).

Though it was not the first women's *anjuman*, by 1922 the PWL was the largest and most representative girl gang on the block. Their stated goals included respecting Islam, promoting girls' education and women's literacy, encouraging national industry and co-ops, caring for orphaned girls, and creating hospitals for impoverished women (they weren't thinking small, that's for sure). Despite attacks by religious conservatives, the PWL focused their campaigns on students, organizing debates, leading literacy classes for adult women, producing fundraiser plays, and, for three years, publishing one of the most successful monthly women's journals in Iran. The paper, *Nesvan Vatankhah* (Patriotic Women), was concerned mostly with social reform; it included articles comparing women's position in Iran to that of post–World War I women around the world, argued hard against low marriage ages, polygamy, and the forced segregation of women; and it straight-up declared that *nothing* could bar women from equality. When reactionary dudes published a pamphlet entitled *Makr-e Zanan* (The Wiles of Women), the PWL collected a bunch of the hateful tracts, marched to what is now Imam Khomeini Square in Tehran, threw them in a pile, and burned them to a crisp.

Whom, exactly, can we thank for such badassery? Well, the founder and first president of the PWL was Mohtaram Eskandari, the daughter of a Qajar prince who wrote extensively on women's rights. Twenty-seven years old when the group was founded in 1922, Mohtaram, who lived with the effects of a spinal injury, was highly educated in history, Persian literature, and

French. (She loved learning so much that she even married her private tutor, the leader of Iran's Socialist Party.) She had been active in the revolution with her father, served as principal of a public girls' school, and became the driving force behind the PWL's establishment and publications. Upon her death at the age of only twenty-nine, from complications of spinal surgery, the PWL was taken over by the member who had spent the most time outside Iran: Mastureh Afshar, a young woman who was also born to Iranian nationalists, never married, had been educated in Russia, and spoke Farsi, Azari, Turkish, and French.

Clearly, the PWL was in capable hands—and not Mastureh's alone. In continuing Mohtaram's mission, Mastureh had the support of some of her best activist buds: Fakhr ol-Ozma Arghun, who edited the journal *Ayandey-e Iran* (Future of Iran) and whose daughter became Iran's greatest modern-day woman poet; Nurol Hoda Manganeh, a writer who went on to edit *Bibi* magazine in 1955; and the writers and activists Safiyeh Eskandari and Homa Mahmudi. Rounding out this girl gang extraordinaire were Fakhr Afagh Parsa and Sediqeh Dowlatabadi. Fakhr was thrown out of the city of Mashad in 1920 for publishing four issues of a journal called *Jahan-e Zanan* (Women's World), making her the first woman editor to be punished in Iran for journalism. Sediqeh, married as a child against her will to an elderly man, not only completed her secondary education in Persian and Arabic but also founded a girls' school, established an *anjuman* and newspaper for women, campaigned to ban imported goods, and appeared in public unveiled. Facing mobs and imprisonment, Sediqeh was banished from her hometown; on her way out, the chief of police who banned her told Sediqeh that she'd been born a century too early. She replied, "I have been born a hundred years too late, otherwise I would have not let women become so enchained by men today." And then she dropped whatever constituted a mic at that time in Iran and headed to Tehran to join forces with the PWL. She attended the International Women's Congress in Berlin in 1922 and went on to study education at the Sorbonne.

The PWL was hardly the only group advocating for women publishing on women's rights in the early twentieth century. There was a proliferation of *anjumans* and publications with fantastic names like "Knowledge," "Blossom," "Women's Voice," "The Women's Freedom Society," and "The National Ladies Society," all with similar goals. A minority of women in Tehran from across all social classes banded together to raise funds for girls' schools and publishing, facing down verbal and physical harassment from a clergy angry at the thought of losing their control of education and social laws. (As many women at the time pointed out, women's education in Iran was far behind that in other Islamic countries like Egypt and Turkey.) Many *anjumans* aligned themselves with socialist political parties, which is not surprising given that Iranian socialism in those days argued for equal rights regardless of gender, race, religion, or ethnicity. As time passed and women were emboldened, their writing moved from nationalism to education to health to straight-up women's rights and politics. And its effects were real: in 1918, a decade after the constitution had mandated girls' education, and before the PWL had even swelled its ranks, the state finally agreed to open public schools for women, a Department of Public Instruction for Women, and a teacher's training college for women. Once the PWL was in full swing, they built on this progress and worked to expand access to education and teaching positions for girls and women across Iran.

A new era began in 1926 in the form of the Pahlavi dynasty, and with it came a whole new set of changes. Its leader, Reza Shah, a military commander, had staged a coup, been elected prime minister, and then established himself as the nation's new monarch, preying on fears of invasion from without and separatists from within. Reza Shah was obsessed with "modernizing" Iran, a term that, to the nearly despotic leader, usually meant "secularizing and westernizing." (For example, he said marriages had to be registered and improved women's education and employment opportunities. But the dude still had four wives and wouldn't let them get divorced, so double standard much?) His time in power led to improvements in technology, infrastructure, economic development, and women's emancipation—but at the cost of the nation's religious, ethnic, and cultural diversity. Persian became the only legal written language, and he fully empowered the military to enforce that and other, new homogenization laws. Basically, Reza Shah tried to take every minority group in Iran and mold them into his vision of a perfect, westernized state.

But the PWL wasn't going anywhere—even when other groups did. By 1932, the PWL was the last major women's *anjuman* standing, and the state was controlled by a guy who did not like any organizations that he didn't control, *especially* not antipatriarchy ones like the PWL. In November and December of that year, the PWL represented Iranian women at the Second Congress of Women of the East, a political summit held mostly in leader Mastureh Afshar's home in Tehran. It drew ladies from Lebanon, Egypt, Iraq, Turkey, and India to discuss shared issues like education and forced polygamy. But after this major event, the shah banned the PWL and all groups like it, establishing instead the government-sanctioned and functionally useless Women's Center, run by his daughter Ashraf Pahlavi, who had exactly zero experience working with or on behalf of Iranian women. (Interesting . . . did she also have a successful handbag line?) The government encouraged a crowd of fanatics to burn the PWL headquarters to the ground, under police supervision. The PWL was officially disbanded.

These events and these women were complicated, and as in many activist spaces, the members of the PWL didn't always agree on everything. Some former members saw the women's movement as over when the PWL was disbanded. Others, like Sediqeh and Mastureh, worked with the Women's Center in an attempt to effect change from inside the system. Some of the PWL hated the veil, seeing it as a symbol of and tool for oppression; others argued that compulsory de-veiling would alienate and divide women by preventing highly religious and lower-income girls from attending public schools (because they couldn't be seen without the covering) and motivate the clergy to fight back even more against women's rights. (Not to mention that de-veiling would represent a kind of capitulation to the imperial influence of the Western world.)

Regardless of the complications, the ladies of the Patriotic

Women's League remain a symbol of hope for women's emancipation even in places and times when change seems impossible. These activists started debates about the most feminist and gender-conscious interpretations of Islam, and these conversations still echo around the world today. Since the 1979 Iranian Revolution and the establishment of the Islamic Republic of Iran, social equality for Iranian women has regressed—but they continue to attend universities, pushing back against bans preventing women from entering certain courses or careers. Though only a quarter of educated Iranian women are currently employed, the women of Iran will never stop fighting for their rights. As Táhirih said, the emancipation of women simply cannot be stopped—no matter how long it takes. ✦

Ruth Bader Ginsburg, Sonia Sotomayor, and Elena Kagan

THE LADIES OF THE US SUPREME COURT

ACTIVE 20TH–21ST CENTURY

In times of darkness and great turmoil, the citizens of the United States look to one band of superheroes to rush in and protect truth, justice, and the American way. No, not the Justice League. Not the Avengers either. Jem and the Holograms? Okay, maybe. But mostly Americans count on protection from the three baddest babes ever to bench: Ruth Bader Ginsburg, Sonia Sotomayor, and Elena Kagan, aka the ladies of SCOTUS.

Like S.H.I.E.L.D. (nothing like S.H.I.E.L.D.) or S.W.O.R.D. (nothing like S.W.O.R.D. either), SCOTUS, the Supreme Court of the United States, protects the rights of the American people by ensuring that laws and citizens conform to the good ol' US Constitution. Established in the third article of that document, SCOTUS is the country's final appeals court for federal law cases. If a case reaches SCOTUS, it's up to these judges to interpret how the Constitution applies to issues that the Founding Fathers were not even remotely close to woke enough to consider, like same-sex marriage, gender and racial equality, and universal healthcare. SCOTUS is an elite gang of nine—to join, you have to be nominated by the president and then confirmed by Senate vote—but once you're in, you're in for life.

Like many well-known supergroups, SCOTUS was an all-dudes affair for quite a while, as in the first 189 years of its existence (interesting, considering their decisions affect the entire US population, which is about fifty-one percent women). In 1981, in an attempt to fulfill a campaign pledge and win back the goodwill of women voters, President Ronald Reagan nominated Sandra "Criminals Are About to Have a Bad" Day O'Connor to the bench, and she was unanimously confirmed by the Senate. (When she moved into her new office, she brought a cushion embroidered with the phrase "Maybe in error but never in doubt." Words to live by.)

By the time O'Connor rode off on her Amazonian mare into the sunset of retirement in 2006, her appointment had opened the door for more women to make their way onto the team. Today, SCOTUS boasts three kick-ass superheroines the country can call on in its time of need.

Ruth Bader Ginsburg

"People ask me sometimes, 'When will there be enough women on the court?' and my answer is, 'When there are nine.'"

The judicial heavy hitter known as Ruth Bader Ginsburg was born Joan Ruth Bader in 1933 to Russian Jewish immigrants in Brooklyn, New York. Supported by an intelligent mother who never got the opportunity to further her own education, Ruth (who went by her middle name to avoid confusion with all the other neighborhood Joans) flew through high school, only to lose her mother to cancer the day before graduation. "I pray that I may be all that she would have been, had she lived in an age when women could aspire and achieve and daughters are cherished as much as sons," Ruth said in a speech at the White House in 1993, the year of her appointment to the Supreme Court.

Dedicated to living the sort of life her mother could not, Ruth worked hard, having heard that many educational institutions likely limited the number of Jewish students they would admit. She was accepted to Cornell University, where she and all the other Jewish female students were assigned rooms in one section of the dormitory. Ruth graduated in 1954 with a B.A. and the best grades for a gal in her class. She was also engaged to Martin Ginsburg. Following her new husband's job to Oklahoma, a 21-year-old Ruth began working at the Social Security Administration, only to be promptly demoted when she chose not to hide her pregnancy. Nice work, 1950s sexism!

Ruth was determined to press forward in her career despite being a young, married, midcentury mother. In 1956 she enrolled at Harvard Law School (maybe you've heard of it), after Martin returned from two years of drafted military service. Ruth was among the roughly 2 percent of women in her class that year, and when the dean asked how Ruth could justify taking a man's spot, she told him she merely wanted to better understand her husband, who was then a second-year law student, also at Harvard. (Sometimes you gotta be the man to beat the man, you know?)

Despite her workload at Harvard, Ruth managed to find time to care for her daughter Jane as well as for Martin, who was fighting testicular cancer. As Ruth explained to NPR in 2016, her husband would eat dinner late (treatment killed his appetite during the day), usually a "bad hamburger" she'd prepared, "and then would dictate to me his senior paper. And then he'd go back to sleep. And it was about 2 [in the morning] when I'd take out the books and start reading what I needed to read to be prepared for classes the next day." After his recovery and graduation, Martin took a job in New York City. Ruth, who had one year of law school to go, transferred to Columbia University, becoming the first woman on staff at both the *Harvard Law Review* and the *Columbia Law Review*. Upon graduation, she tied for valedictorian.

Though she struggled at first to find law work and respect (the Supreme Court judge for whom she wanted to clerk rejected her because of her gender), Ruth racked up experience and sharpened her skills. She worked for the Southern District Court of New York; served as associate director of Columbia's Project on International Procedure; taught law at Rutgers and Columbia (becoming the first tenured female professor at Columbia, though she was paid less than her male colleagues because, as she was told, "your husband has a very good job"); was a fellow at the interdisciplinary Center for Advanced Study in the Behavioral Sciences at Stanford; and, at age 47, became a judge in the Washington DC Court of Appeals. Oh, and she also cofounded the Women's Rights Project of the American Civil Liberties Union, where she served as general counsel on over three hundred gender discrimination cases, including six that were taken all the way up to the Supreme Court (five of which she won). Janet Reno, then US attorney general, recommended that President Bill Clinton nominate Ruth to fill a vacancy on the Supreme Court. Ruth was confirmed by an almost unanimous vote and was sworn in on August 3, 1993, at age 60. She was the first Democratic presidential appointment to the Court in over twenty-five years, the first Jewish Supreme Court justice since 1969, and the second woman to sit on the SCOTUS bench ever.

Which is all pretty dang inspirational, but it gets even better when you consider that, to this day, Ruth is still standing up for the rights of women and the marginalized whenever she believes the Constitution supports it (which is, you know, a lot). Considered the most liberal Supreme Court judge, Ruth believes that "women belong in all places where decisions are being made," and she has done a good job of making sure she's heard—even when subjected to "hepeating." "I don't know how many meetings I attended in the '60s and the '70s, where I would say something, and I thought it was a pretty good idea," Ruth told *USA Today* in 2009. "Then somebody else would say exactly what I said. Then people would become alert to it, respond to it."

Ruth has become particularly outspoken on the court since Sandra Day O'Connor's retirement, dissenting on rulings that undermine equality for people regardless of gender as well as fighting to defend the Voting Rights Act, affirmative action, and access to contraception. She believes that "we should not be held back from pursuing our full talents, from contributing what we could contribute to the society, because we fit into a certain mold—because we belong to a group that historically has been the object of discrimination." Ruth broadcasts that message loud and clear—she carries a tote bag with her face printed on one side and the words "I Dissent" on the other. She's the Notorious RBG, and she's here to help.

Sonia Sotomayor

> *"Personal experiences affect the facts that judges choose to see. My hope is that I will take the good from my experiences and extrapolate them further into areas with which I am unfamiliar."*

Sonia Maria Sotomayor, the first woman of color to sit on the SCOTUS bench, was born in 1954 to Puerto Rican parents who had moved to the Bronx during World War II. (Sonia has been known to identify as Nuyorican, a portmanteau of Puerto Rican and New Yorker.) Her young life wasn't easy: she grew up in tenements and in the projects, was diagnosed with diabetes at age 8, and lost her father by age 9. Still, she had big plans. Inspired by Nancy Drew, this "child with dreams," as she later described herself, knew by 10 years old that she wanted to go to law school. She had the encouragement of her mother, who worked six days a week as a nurse to make ends meet. "She had almost a fanatical emphasis on education," Sonia said of her mother to the *New York Times* in 1992. "We got encyclopedias, and she struggled to make those payments. She kept saying, 'I don't care what you do, but be the best at it.'"

Sonia took the first step toward that law career in 1972 when she graduated as her high school's valedictorian. With a full scholarship in hand, thanks to her grades and an affirmative action policy (instituted to correct for cultural bias in standardized testing), Sonia headed to Princeton University, which had started accepting women only three years earlier and where the total number of Latinx students was in the mere double digits. She studied hard and joined Princeton's Puerto Rican students' association, Acción Puertorriqueña, focusing much of her activism on urging the university to hire more Latinx professors and offer more classes on Latin American studies (hoping to increase both from zero, to be perfectly clear). After the university's Puerto Rican and Chicano students filed an official complaint about "an institutional pattern of discrimination," Sonia wrote an opinion piece for the *Daily Princetonian* on May 10, 1974. "It has been said that the universities of America are the vanguard of societal ideas and changes," she wrote. "Princeton University claims to foster the intellectual diversity, spirit and thoughts that are necessary components in order to achieve this ideal. Yet words are transitory, it is the practice of the ideas you espouse that affect society and are permanent."

Always an active community member, Sonia somehow found time to work off campus, running an after-school program for children at Princeton's Third World Center and volunteering as a Spanish-language interpreter at a local psychiatric hospital. She graduated cum laude in 1976 and was awarded the Pyne Prize, Princeton's highest general distinction for undergraduates. The *Daily Princetonian* noted that, although Sonia's grades were spectacular, she was remarkable for "her dedication to the life of minority students at Princeton."

Thanks to another well-deserved scholarship, Sonia enrolled at Yale Law School, where she was an editor of the *Yale Law Journal* and *Yale Journal of International Law* and kept up her Latinx-focused community activism. Yet still she faced discrimination. At a job-recruitment dinner during the school year, a partner at a Washington DC law firm wondered to her face if she had gotten into Yale only because she was Puerto Rican. She filed an official complaint against him with a student-faculty tribunal, and the firm apologized to her—in the *Washington Post*. Dang.

Clearly, Sonia was a most impressive job candidate, and sure enough, upon graduation from Yale in 1979, she went straight to work for the New York district attorney's office. Five years later, she made her way to a boutique law firm, where she became partner in 1988, transitioning smoothly from homicides to handbag fraud. Once, in a real superhero moment, a motorbike-riding Sonia chased down escaping Chinatown counterfeiters, which may just be the raddest thing a lawyer has ever done in the pursuit of justice.

Sonia served for five years on the board of the State of New York Mortgage Agency, supporting affordable housing, and in 1992 she was appointed to the New York District Court, making her the first Latinx federal judge in state history. *New York Times* reporter James C. McKinley Jr. wrote in 1995 that Sonia had gained "a reputation as a sharp, outspoken and fearless jurist, someone who does not let powerful interests bully, rush or cow her into a decision." (People especially liked her for bringing an end to the Major League Baseball strike that year.) In 1998, President Bill Clinton nominated Sonia to the US Court of Appeals for the Second Circuit, where she would rule on cases in the states of Connecticut, New York, and Vermont. Once confirmed, she became a member of the Second Circuit Task Force on Gender, Racial, and Ethnic Fairness in the Courts. In May 2009, President Barack Obama said to a room full of reporters that he wanted a Supreme Court nominee with experience. He elaborated: "Experience being tested by obstacles and barriers, by hardship and misfortune; experience insisting, persisting, and ultimately overcoming those barriers. It is experience that can give a person a common touch and a sense of compassion, an understanding of how the world works and how ordinary people live." He nominated Sonia, and she was confirmed in August.

Despite this very-big-deal position (not to mention her degrees from some of the best schools in the country), Sonia has never lost her passion for the people. She's celebrated New Year's Eve watching the ball drop in New York City; been interviewed by Oprah and Katie Couric; thrown first pitches at baseball games; written a *New York Times* best-selling memoir; and even appeared on *Sesame Street*. She regularly brings national attention to racial profiling and the Black Lives Matter movement. She keeps candy in her office, both to balance her blood sugar and to encourage people to "come talk to [her] more." She was the first person ever to say "undocumented immigrant" instead of "illegal immigrant" in a Supreme Court opinion. And she is absolutely a hero.

Elena Kagan

"You want a court of people who really care about law and are good at doing it and are experienced at doing it and who bring that worldview even to cases that involve matters of broad principle."

The third lady justice in our trio, Elena Kagan also hails from New York City. She was born in 1960 to a teacher and a lawyer living on the Upper West Side, and she started arguing for her rights at a young age. She clashed with her rabbi over her bat mitzvah celebration (the rabbi had never performed one, and Elena felt that the coming-of-age occasion for girls should be celebrated in her synagogue, just as it was for boys). She enrolled at the prestigious, merit-based Hunter College High School, and it's safe to say she knew exactly what she wanted from her future. Her classmates remember Elena wanting to be a US Supreme Court justice even then. In her 1977 senior yearbook, she appears in a photo wearing a judge's robe and holding a gavel; the photo is paired with a quote from Supreme Court justice Felix Frankfurter.

Once Elena put her mind to something, nothing could stop her (clearly, because she did eventually make it to the US Supreme Court). At Princeton University, just a few years after her bud-to-be Sonia Sotomayor, Elena studied the history of socialism in twentieth-century New York City while also serving as an editor at the *Daily Princetonian*, a position she leveraged to call for more transparency in the school's governing processes. She graduated cum laude with a Bachelor of Arts degree in 1981, then headed to Oxford University on a fellowship to continue her education. After grabbing a Master of Philosophy degree in politics in 1983, she earned her doctorate in law (cum laude, of course, in 1986) from Harvard Law School, where she made law review just as RBG had before her. With this impressive set of degrees under her belt, she clerked for the DC Court of Appeals and then a year later, in 1988, for Supreme Court justice Thurgood Marshall (who called her "Shorty," something that is pretty hilarious to imagine coming out of Thurgood Marshall's mouth).

Elena spent a brief two years in private practice at a DC law firm before joining the University of Chicago Law School as a professor in 1991—the same year as another upcoming lawyer and lecturer named Barack Obama. (Maybe you've heard of him.) While she worked, Elena continued to write; her students were particularly interested in her takes on free speech in the *Supreme Court Review* and the *University of Chicago Law Review*. For a short time in 1993, Elena served as special counsel to the US Senate Judiciary Committee to advise President Clinton on his Supreme Court nominee. At just 33 years old, Elena sat in on the confirmation hearing, led by committee chair Senator Joe

Biden, and listened to Ruth Bader Ginsburg say that she imagined seeing a SCOTUS made up of "three, four, perhaps even more" women in her lifetime. (Spoiler alert: she's gotten really close.)

Elena eventually gave up tenure at the University of Chicago and headed back to DC, becoming President Clinton's Associate White House Counsel in 1995 and Deputy Assistant to the President for Domestic Policy in 1997. Next, she popped back in to academia at Harvard Law School, first as a visiting professor, then as full professor, before becoming the school's first female dean in 2003 (no big deal). In her time at Harvard, she improved faculty relationships, campus facilities, and the overall student experience by doing everything from offering free morning coffee to banning the military from recruiting on campus because of their homophobic "don't ask, don't tell" policy. You know, normal stuff.

In 2009, President Obama nominated Elena for solicitor general, aka the person who represents the federal government in Supreme Court cases, making her the first woman ever to get that gig. Another nomination, this time for Supreme Court justice, came a year later. Sixty-nine law school deans from around the country wrote an open letter in support of her nomination, and she was confirmed in August 2010. With Elena on the bench, SCOTUS reached a landmark one-third-women milestone.

Elena Kagan is known as a bridge builder, a good listener, and a person focused on improving relationships, no matter the issue. Seriously: she had the first-ever frozen yogurt machine installed in the Supreme Court cafeteria (the newest justice is always appointed to the cafeteria committee, where, Elena told *Business Insider* in 2017, they "have to spend an hour every month thinking about the chocolate-chip cookies," among other things). Also, her writing is funny as heck, and she has consistently stood up for women's rights on the bench. Give 'em hell, Justice.

The Supremes Unite!

These women are amazing on their own, but when their judicial superpowers combine, they become the Voltron of powerful female friendship. The most impressive thing (okay, one of *many* impressive things) about the SCOTUS squad is that they've become friends even though their political views (and interests) differ. Although Ruth, Sonia, and Elena share a few things in common—all are from New York City, were nominated by Democratic presidents, and are champions of women's issues—it is their differences that make them even more awesome.

To wit: Elena used to play softball and Sonia loves the Yankees, but Ruth couldn't pretend to care about sports if you paid her. Whereas Ruth raised two kids with a supportive husband who split housework and other chores evenly, neither Sonia nor Elena had children. The three justices share lunch breaks in the cafeteria, where they talk about museum exhibits, music, and books, but never ongoing cases. Both Elena and Sonia wore a bright-blue blazer and black blouse to the first day of their confirmation hearings (twinsies!), and in her official Supreme Court portrait, Sonia wears a special jabot (the frilly collar worn by justices over their robes) that was a gift from Ruth. At Sonia's first end-of-term party, just days after Ruth's husband Martin's death,

Sonia convinced Ruth to salsa with her on the dance floor because Martin would have wanted her to; after that special moment, Ruth held Sonia's cheeks and thanked her.

Of the trio's connection, Elena has said, "There are nine of us, and we do this thing that only the nine of us do, which you can't really talk to anybody else about. There's a kind of bonding that occurs because of that." This bond is apparent in the courtroom: Ruth usually asks the first question, Sonia the most questions, and Elena the best questions, making them a well-balanced team, and they agree with one another in more than 93 percent of cases. They are also constantly and frustratingly interrupted by male colleagues, something Sonia and Ruth have learned to work around by cutting phrases like "sorry," "excuse me," and "may I ask" from their vocabulary.

Delightfully, Elena and Ruth even share a personal trainer: "He tells me [that Elena] has the best jab-cross-hook-punch combination on the federal bench," Ruth told Adam Liptak of the *New York Times* in 2014. The admiration goes both ways: at an annual lecture in Ruth's honor that same year, Elena credited her friend with "chang[ing] the face of antidiscrimination law," mentioning Ruth's dissent written for *Ledbetter v. Goodyear Tire and Rubber Company*, which Elena called "the most effective dissent of this generation." That case led to the Lilly Ledbetter Fair Pay Act of 2009, a landmark piece of legislation in the fight for women's equal pay.

Despite an acronym rivaling that of their fictional crime-busting counterparts, the women of SCOTUS are vitally important to the current generation of girls, specifically because they aren't superheroes: they're smart, motivated women who fought their way through a sexist and discriminatory system to effect change from the inside out. They are strong-willed and steadfast leaders whose very existence dissents from the way the world has been run for the last two thousand years—and affirms what the future should be. "That is the dissenter's hope, that they are writing not for today but tomorrow," Ruth has said. That's something worth fighting for—especially with your gals by your side. ✦

CHAPTER 3

WARRIOR SQUADS

W hat book of badass lady teams would be complete without women warriors? Women have taken up arms throughout history for their country, for their family, and just for fun. Let's take a look at four of the most wicked warrior squads from around the globe.

The Dahomey "Amazons"

THE ROYAL REGIMENT THAT
ASTOUNDED THE WORLD

ACTIVE CIRCA 1645–1890

The first twenty minutes of Patty Jenkins's amazing and long-
long-awaited 2016 movie *Wonder Woman*, featuring Diana and
her women warriors living in relative peace and harmony, all of
them buff and tough and awesome, is enough to make you wish
that the island of Themyscira was real. Although the Amazons of
the DC Comics universe are fictitious, real Amazons did indeed
exist, waging war under the command of other ladies. The band
that most resembled the Grecian fighters of myth, according to
those lucky enough to witness them in action, was the women
fighters of the African kingdom of Dahomey, and they could seriously mess you up if you disagreed.

To understand the Amazons, first you have to understand

Dahomey, a kingdom that existed from the 1600s to the end of the 1800s on West Africa's southern shore of the Gulf of Guinea (roughly where modern-day Benin is). In the early 1600s, about the same time the *Mayflower* was docking in North America, the Fon people (who still inhabit Benin today) moved east from neighboring Togo and established the seat of their monarchy in a town called Abomey, about seventy miles north of the coastline. A centralized government and a permanent military were established around their king, and quickly the new kingdom became focused on one goal: expansion. Their land in the Dahomey territory was plateaus, rivers, and swamps, all of which were bad for farming and generally low on natural resources. To survive, the people of Dahomey would have to rely on neighbors (and by "rely on," I mean "conquer and rule").

Besides battling with other kingdoms, the other thing Dahomey did best (read: cruelly) was slavery; the abundance of prisoners of war combined with their West African coastal location made Dahomey the largest port on the continent for the slave trade. More than a million people were sold into bondage there between the seventeenth and nineteenth centuries. To protect its political and economic power, Dahomey was heavily militarized, and no one was exempt from pitching in to the war effort—not even women.

There's no consensus on the exact origin of the warrior women, but a few oral traditions offer possible explanations. In one account, King Houegbadja (aka Wegbaja, aka Aho, depending on whom you ask), who reigned from the mid- to late 1600s, formed the *gbeto*, a band of women hunters, to provide him with elephant meat and ivory. Another story says that Houegbadja's successor, King Akaba, had a twin sister, Ahangbé, who acted as co-ruler and had her own palace and court. (The Fon people worshipped twins and thought they had a special connection to the spirit world, including the ability to come back to life after death.) When King Akaba died potentially of smallpox in the midst of conquering some folks (oral tradition is unclear as to who, exactly), Ahangbé took his place on the battlefield. After her victory, Ahangbé ruled briefly as regent, becoming the first and most prominent of Dahomey's women warriors (she has since been stricken from the official record, either because of politics or because she was a woman).

Another (and more credible, according to some scholars) version concerns the many wives, or *ahosi*, of the twins' successor, King Agaja. To prevent a potential coup, the *ahosi* were the only people allowed to live in the palace; according to legend, the women wore the king's weapons to show them off to his visitors. From there, they could have become soldiers. Finally, it's also possible that some combination of all these accounts is true.

Regardless of the specifics, by the nineteenth century Dahomey's dual government/military system boasted some gender parity—for every male official or officer, a woman held equal rank and title. Allowing women to be warriors just made sense; between the wars, the slave trade, and the men sent to the neighboring Oyo Empire in tribute, the kingdom simply didn't have enough dudes to do the fighting. Dahomey's women did most of the physical labor anyway—farming, harvesting, carrying water, spinning, pottery making, processing palm oil, and trading goods at market—so they were more than physically capable of fighting. In fact, many Amazon war songs reference the warriors' early days in the field in lyrics like

> *Let the men harvest the manioc! . . .*
> *Men, men, stay!*
> *Let the men stay at home!*
> *Let them grow maize*
> *And cultivate palm trees . . .*
> *We, we will go to war.*

The Dahomey Amazons came from varied circumstances. Some were captured slaves and prisoners from other nations; some were criminals conscripted into service; some were high-born girls given as gifts to the king; some were lower-class volunteers; and some were just mouthy wives and misbehaving daughters. By 1818, when Agaja's successor, King Gezo, took the throne, he was so impressed by the women's ferocity that he initiated serious recruiting efforts, skyrocketing the warriors' numbers into the thousands. Every three years, the king sent out a representative called a *kpakpa* to find the strongest girls in every village, and, according to Western observers, "each private person" had to give up one of their daughters for palace service. Back at the palace, the girls were assigned different status levels depending on where they came from. Rich girls might be part of the harem or officers, whereas the daughters of slaves might become palace slaves. Once recruited, the Amazons took a sacred oath, drinking their shared blood out of a polished human skull to bind them while promising they would never betray their warrior sisters.

No matter where the Amazons had come from, Dahomey held them in almost worshipful esteem. The women lived in palaces exclusively with other Amazons, didn't have to do housework or cooking, and could spend their downtime however they wanted. As *ahosi* they were sworn to celibacy, but the vow was less about taboos or controls over women's sexuality than about preventing emotional connections and pregnancy—which, of course, would interfere with their fighting. And if the warriors broke their vow, they were rarely punished harshly (with some exceptions, mostly to serve as examples). In his 1864 book on Dahomey, Richard Burton—an East India Company captain, explorer, translator, spy, writer, fencer, epic-mustache-haver, and, according to some modern-day scholars, a "passionate racist"— wrote that he saw around 150 pregnant Amazons, some of whom were said to be the daughters of other Amazons.

In close combat, the Amazons were fearsome with a rifle or a knife, and their diverse specialized units were instrumental in combat. The *gbeto*, the oldest and most respected unit, wore distinctive antlered iron crowns; they existed well into the 1800s, disbanding only when they had hunted the area's elephants to extinction. Other units were made up of rifle specialists, archers, and what Burton called "razor women," those who carried a weapon resembling a three-foot, twenty-pound foldable straight razor. All of the Amazons were particularly skilled in hand-to-hand combat, oiling up their bods and sharpening their teeth and fingernails before hardening them with brine for maximum damage potential. When the warriors went out into town, a girl would precede the group ringing a bell to announce their arrival; all men were required to get out of their way and were forbidden to look at them (goals). Touching an Amazon meant an instant death penalty. Accounts by Western dudes gripe about this arrangement: Burton wrote that having to avoid the Amazons' path was one of Dahomey's "greatest nuisances," and J. Alfred Skertchly, an insect scientist with the last name of a Roald Dahl character, wrote in his 1874 account of his eight months in Dahomey that he "continually" was forced to take a "side to path" path "instead of making a straight course."

These narratives underscore the complicated fact that most of what we know about the Amazons of Dahomey was recorded by outsiders—namely, white dudes who traveled to Africa. (The first interview with a Dahomey woman wouldn't be conducted until the 1920s, long after their heyday.) The first recorded sighting of Dahomey's women warriors by a foreigner was in 1724, when Bulfinch Lamb (real name), an agent of the British Royal African Company, found himself in captivity in Dahomey and wrote to his boss about his experiences. A few years later, in 1727, William Snelgrave (also real, somehow), an English slave trader, saw four women holding muskets behind King Agaja; he later wrote that, during a skirmish with the Oyo Empire, the monarch "ordered a great number of Women to be armed like Soldiers, and appointed Officers to each Company, with Colours, Drums and Umbrellas" to intimidate the enemy. Nearly forty years later, the head of a nearby French fort, Antoine-Edmé Pruneau de Pommegorge (that's "Prune of Applethroat," if you're counting), wrote that the king was guarded by "two or three thousand" wives. Several of these eighteenth-century dudes describe flashy, dazzling parades in which teenage women warriors, armed with muskets and short swords, would march in formation behind a commander, naked from the waist up like their male counterparts. The first person to compare Dahomey's women warriors—an "unusual spectacle" and a "novelty in modern history"—with the Amazons of ancient legend was Archibald Dalzel (a Scot we would probably at one time have called an adventurer, but now can pretty safely call an imperialist colonialist slave trader toolbag for his belief that enslaving African people was a way to "save" them from a life of barbarism). He wrote in 1793 that several hundred women in Dahomey's palaces were "trained to the use of arms, under a female general and subordinate officers, appointed by the King."

European writers were also fascinated by the women's clothes and ornaments. Scottish traveler John Duncan described them in 1845 as wearing blue-and-white striped cotton sleeveless tunics that fell to their knees (both men and women started wearing shirts around 1830, probably because of European influence), with short pants visible for two inches below that, all held together around the waist by a cartouche box, a kind of ammunition pouch. They wore caps, whose color and logo differed by unit— some had crocodiles, crosses, sharks, or turtles. Queen Victoria even sent Gezo a gift of two thousand war caps for the Amazons in 1847. Skertchly described the women as "profusely ornamented with magic relics" to help in warfare—though their weapons probably helped, too. The warriors used everything from guns to knives to swords (basically, whatever had been popular in Europe a few decades earlier and then imported to Africa) and were well trained in all of them. Visitors in the 1850s recalled seeing shooting demonstrations and mock wars, in which the Amazons were the best shots and fiercest fighters. French naval officer Jean Bayol remembered one warrior called Nanisca who would squeeze the blood of her enemies off her weapon and swallow it, an example of some of the terrifying tactics King Glele (Gezo's successor) encouraged in order to intimidate potential enemies.

And although Western writers definitely used the kind of racist garbage language you might expect ("fearfully savage and bloodthirsty," "purely animal—bestial," etc.), their writings also reveal their own kind of admiration. Edmond Chaudoin, a Fabre & Co. trading manager who was held prisoner in Dahomey in the late 1800s, wrote that the women fighters were "as full of muscle as the male warriors," with attitude "as well disciplined and correct" as the men. "Such are the amazons under arms," he wrote, "differing very much from the savage horde which fantasy has painted them." Richard Burton of the epic 'stache said the Amazons enjoyed greater status than the men of the Dahomey court, though the women would frequently say they were "no longer females but males," having taken up the warrior mantle. (This may be the nineteenth-century equivalent of the backhanded compliment "she's not like other girls," but hey, it's something.) In the 1850s John Duncan the Scotsman even made a personal connection by befriending a tall, quiet 22-year-old Amazon called Adadimo, who had risen quickly in the ranks for taking male prisoners during military campaigns.

By the mid-nineteenth century, Gezo's army included nearly six thousand Amazons, about 4 percent of the Dahomey population. But as their numbers grew, so did their casualties. Ill-fated fights against the walled Nigerian city of Abeokuta in 1851 and 1864 saw almost a thousand Amazons perish; a smallpox epidemic reduced their numbers further, to about one thousand to three thousand in the second half of the nineteenth century, just when they had become infamous the world over. The Amazons remained active until the 1890s, when the French took control of the kingdom, despite the best efforts of Dahomey's toughest warriors—women included, naturally. Still, the Amazons were said to have been the last to surrender. French officers recalled the women as "remarkable for their courage and their ferocity," with "prodigious bravery" and "extreme valor." (They were also straight-up badass: in 1892, the French found a clay relief drawing of Amazons boiling enemy corpses in a kettle resting on a skull, probably so they could use their bones for trophies.)

Today, only a handful of historians (as in, like, five) have made it their mission to bring to light as much information about the Dahomey Amazons as they can. Despite the scholarly differences of opinion typical in modern academia, we can be certain that the Amazons were real, they were fierce, and they proved early on that women could be just as tough as, if not tougher than, men. Through centuries when women across the globe had few rights and little respect, the women warriors of Dahomey captured the world's imagination. Without a doubt, as a kingdom, Dahomey perpetrated and profited from the most despicable acts imaginable. But the Dahomey Amazons are proof that, even in the most heinous circumstances, a group of strong women can exemplify strength, bravery, and leadership. ✦

Anne Bonny and Mary Read

THE LADY PIRATES WHO RULED THE HIGH SEAS

ACTIVE CIRCA 1698–1721

In November 1720, two young women—best friends, both pregnant, in their mid-twenties—sat across from each other. Hours earlier, they had been standing together looking out over the rails of their ship, enjoying the bright Jamaican sun glinting off the sea, warming their faces. Now, they were feet apart, separated by concrete and bars. They were in jail, and they were going to be hanged for piracy.

Or were they?

Here's an interesting line you can use at parties: the pirates of pop culture that we know and love, who pillaged and murdered and caused trouble for colonialists in the Caribbean for countless years, really existed for an incredibly short period. In fact, the "pirates" you think of when I say "pirates" operated only from about 1696 to 1732, and their "golden age" lasted just one decade: 1715 to 1725. And despite their bad rep, golden age pirates were actually a subversive and revolutionary movement of democracy and independence that welcomed all kinds into its ranks. Yes, even women.

In early eighteenth-century Europe, maritime activity was a crucial part of life. Britain, France, and Spain were in full swing establishing colonies in the New World, and the Atlantic Ocean was bustling with vessels—not just navy ships defending colonial interests, but commercial ships engaged in business in the New World. London got its tea from India, its sugar from the West Indies, and its labor from captured Africans forced onto ships as human cargo to await enslavement. Even the flow of information was conducted by ships that carried letters from continent to continent.

All this sailing required literal hands on deck. The Royal Navy was so desperate for bodies to work their ships that government-sanctioned press gangs started popping up in British port cities, kidnapping able-bodied men and forcing (or "pressing") them onto ships for service. And these vessels, whether they belonged to the Royal Navy or to the Dutch West India Company, were run militaristically; all-white, all-male crews obeyed their captains or stood trial for mutiny. Their life was one of back-breaking labor, hauling cargo and sails and rigging, without understanding of the health issues that accompany living and working in close quarters on the high seas, like skin cancer and sunburns caused by reflected glare, or germ theory, or actually getting scurvy. Needless to say, these seafaring fellows tended to be pretty unhappy with their gig.

Enter: pirates. Independent vessels whose captains vowed fealty to no nation, pirate ships were a seafaring extension of some of the more radical ideas that had started to take hold in both the Old and New Worlds: independence, freedom, self-governance, and self-made wealth. (Spoiler alert: the American and French Revolutions were a-brewin' based on these same notions.) For sailors who wanted to take to the sea and maybe make a living out of it, piracy was ultra-tempting. The golden age saw about twenty to thirty pirate commodores in action, with a few thousand crew behind them—but even these seemingly small numbers were enough to bring nations to their knees. Patrolling the West Indies and routes back to the Old World, pirate ships halted trade, communication, and commerce. But they didn't do so out of some anarchist, sociopathic love of murder and mayhem.

Contrary to the popular image, which was originally promoted by European governments actively seeking to cast pirates unfavorably, they were actually, often, surprisingly ... good dudes. They'd help other pirate ships. They'd attack slave ships and offer a life of freedom on the seas to captured Africans. They disrupted the very nature of colonialism. And people *liked* it. The pirates had a lot of fans, especially in the colonies, where they were viewed as exciting and liberating heroes of the common people. Which makes sense, especially when you know that these mariners were much more about stealing from the rich (slave owners; colonialists) and giving to the poor (themselves) than about causing senseless chaos.

Usually made up of defected English or Irish sailors, pirate crews also had Scottish, French, Danish, Swedish, African, and Native American seamen, many of whom were escaping painful lives of enslavement, indentured servitude, or poverty. Away from oppressive captains and company owners, pirates ran their ships democratically, voting on leaders and difficult decisions, splitting bounty equally, and even providing disability benefits in the not uncommon case of on-the-job injury. When pirates boarded naval vessels, men would come over willingly; escaped slaves made up about a quarter of many pirate crews. Pirate ships were a place where the down and out and unwanted could find a new way up in the world.

Among such folks were (you guessed it) women, especially from the working classes. In the mid-1700s, despite all the talk of individual liberties, men still literally wore the pants. So it's not surprising that tales of cross-dressing women started to become a Big Thing. And these stories were based in reality: cross-dressing was often a viable way for working-class women to change their circumstances since, in a lot of cases, the only qualification they lacked for a particular job was literally wearing pants. Especially popular at this time were the stories of Hannah Snell, a woman who became a soldier while searching for the man who abandoned her when she was pregnant with his child, and Ann Mills, who fought in the War of Austrian Succession dressed as a man. But countless other women whose names we don't know did the same, such as the more than one hundred recorded instances of women dressed as men working for the Dutch East India Company. People weren't shaming these gals, either: in 1762, one essayist wrote that there were so many more women in Britain than men due to war that it only made sense to give women their own naval units. (Though he said "those who are fit to bear children, are likewise fit to bear arms," he also suggested they wear pink satin vests with white feather hats; so close, my dude.) Still more women (both in and out of pants) boarded ships as fishers, servants, cooks, and companions and worked as merchants and traders along the coasts. Some even got in on that sweet swashbuckling life, like Gráinne O'Malley, an Irishwoman who became a revolutionary and "pirate queen."

It's probably a story like Gráinne's that inspired Anne Bonny, born just outside Cork, Ireland, in 1698. Anne's father, probably a lawyer named William Cormac, had a good law practice and a solid reputation, and Mary Brennan, Anne's mother, was his maid. Everyone in the village knew that Mary had given birth to a girl—and that William already had a wife—so William dressed Anne up as a boy to maintain his image, claiming that Anne was in fact the son of a relative training to be his clerk. William's wife, who was no fool, quickly discovered the ruse and wanted nothing to do with him. William and Mary moved in together, which caused such a scandal that he was forced to shutter his practice and move with Anne and Mary to South Carolina.

Though Mary died in 1710, William did well for himself in the colonies, earning enough money as a merchant to buy a plantation. Anne, already "robust" and of "fierce and courageous temper," ran William's household and took care of herself, once avoiding a would-be sexual assault by beating the guy so badly "that he lay ill of it a considerable time." When she was 20 years old, against her father's wishes, Anne married James Bonny, a sailor who "was not worth a groat." Though we can't be certain of her motivations, Anne might have been dissatisfied with the expectations placed on her by her father, unwilling to take part in the ownership of enslaved workers, unhappy with a potential suitor, or hungry for the wild adventures enjoyed by those cross-dressing women of popular ballads. Her father disowned her, and the newlyweds took off for Nassau on the island of New Providence, in the Bahamas, hoping to find work. But Anne was about to find a lot more than just a job.

In the notorious pirate haven of the Bahamas, Anne met the tall, dark-eyed, and handsome John Rackam. At various taverns, John told Anne about his life: that he'd been a quartermaster for the famous pirate Charles Vane; that he'd been elected captain when Vane showed signs of cowardice; that his crew had come to Nassau to take advantage of King George I's offer to pardon all surrendering pirates; that he was better known as "Calico Jack" for his brightly patterned clothes. Anne fell for Jack and for the life he offered her. She abandoned her husband and set out aboard the pirate's ship, where, against all odds, she would soon find herself face-to-face with another cross-dressing lady pirate: Mary Read.

Mary was born around 1695, just outside of London. Her mother had been married to, and had a son with, a sailor with the last name Read, but both father and son had died at sea. To hide the shame of her illegitimate daughter, and to keep money coming from her in-laws, Mary's mother decided to pass her daughter off as her dead older brother, which probably didn't cause a weird dynamic at home at all, I'm sure. By age 13, Mary was "growing bold and strong," and her "roving mind" (and probably a desire to escape poverty) led her to enroll as a soldier on a man-of-war, still living as a boy. Mary served in the British infantry and cavalry in Flanders, where she fell in love with, and later married, a fellow soldier. Together they ran a pub in the Netherlands until her husband's untimely death, at which point Mary threw her pants back on and went off in search of her next adventure. After rejoining the army briefly, she took a post as a sailor on a Dutch merchant's ship headed for the West Indies. This being the golden age of pirates, it didn't take long before Mary's ship was beset, and she willingly switched crews to work under the Jolly Roger. Piracy was her best chance at a free life. Mary's ship headed for Nassau to take advantage of George I's pirate pardon, and that's where she ran headlong into Calico Jack. And Anne Bonny.

Anne and Mary had an immediate connection, though both were dressed as men. According to the most famous contemporaneous account of the duo, Anne, "who was not altogether so reserved in point of chastity, took a particular liking to [Mary]; in short, Anne Bonny took her for a handsome young fellow." Anne told Mary she was a girl. After a pause, Mary—to Anne's "great disappointment"—revealed the same. Calico Jack, so "disturb'd" by the instant "intimacy" between Anne and Mary, threatened that "he would cut [Anne's] new lover's throat," so they let him in on the secret.

Now, with two kick-ass gal pals in his crew of a dozen or so, Calico Jack returned to the seas. Jack kept both his crew and his bounties small, mostly stealing from fishing ships and merchant sloops around Cuba, Haiti, Bermuda, and Jamaica before setting the captives free. Anne and Mary were two of the bravest, brashest, and boldest members of his crew. Former captives testified about the women's actions at their trial in 1720, with many expressing similar sentiments: that Anne and Mary "were very active" and "were both very profligate, cursing, and swearing much, and ready and willing to do any thing on board." Clearly there "of their own free-will and consent," Anne and Mary were not "kept, or detain'd by force"; rather, the women were having a grand ol' time destroying colonialist trade routes *and* concepts of racial and gender hierarchies in one fell swoop. Mostly, they wore women's clothes on deck, unless they were attacked, in which case they'd don men's attire as a show of force. One former woman captive, Dorothy Thomas, later said that Anne and Mary "wore men's jackets, and long trousers, and handkerchiefs tied about their heads, and that each of them had a machete and pistol in their hands." She complained that Anne and Mary had argued she should be killed "to prevent her coming against them in court." (They weren't wrong, I guess?) Eventually, having eloped with Jack at sea, Anne became pregnant. She returned landside to a little homestead they kept in Cuba to give birth and then headed out again with the gang. Mary fell in love with a (male) pirate, whose life she once saved from certain death in a duel against a pirate with deadly aim; she scheduled her own duel with the same pirate two hours before her lover was meant to fight him and killed him "on the spot." And for all the freedoms they enjoyed, let's not forget that Mary and Anne weren't simply gallivanting around the seas together. They were doing hard manual labor to pursue and maintain a life free from societal expectations.

Alas, their fantastic exploits and fabulous friendship couldn't last forever. In August 1720, Anne, Mary, and the gang stole the twelve-ton, six-gun sloop *William* from Nassau harbor and took it out to do more pirating. But the British government, finally tired of the shenanigans and multiple stolen ships, had started to crack down on piracy. The governor of the Bahamas issued a warrant for Calico Jack's arrest. By October, the British privateer Captain Jonathan Barnet had found them, and when he and his crew boarded the *William*, Anne and Mary were heroes once again. According to a contemporary account, "no body was more forward or courageous than [Anne], and particularly when they were taken, she and Mary Read, with one more, were all the persons that durst keep the deck." Everyone else hid belowdecks. Mary fired a shot into the hold and berated them for their cowardice—the ultimate insult among pirates. By the time Anne and Mary's trial began on November 28, eighteen members of Jack's crew had already been hanged from the Nassau port walls to serve as examples. Anne said that if Jack had fought like a man, maybe he wouldn't have hung like a dog. Both pregnant, Anne and Mary "pleaded their bellies" in the hopes that they would convince the court to grant them mercy, though Mary said that "men of courage" such as they didn't fear the gallows. Mary died of fever in prison the following April. Genealogical research by Anne's likely descendants suggests that her father rescued her from prison and that in April 1721 she gave birth in Jamaica to a boy she named John. Anne's father shipped her back to Charles Town (i.e., Charleston, South Carolina), where she married Joseph Burleigh that December. Anne's life stayed exciting in its own way: she and Joseph would go on to have eight kids together. She died in 1782, a well-respected, eighty-four-year-old woman.

Anne and Mary's story is an amazing, almost unbelievable account of two lady friends crushing it in the heyday of piracy. Lucky for us, their tale is definitely legit, corroborated by several independent sources from the time. We have the September 5, 1720, proclamation from Woodes Rogers, the royal governor of the Bahamas, that demands the arrest of Jack's crew and names each member, including the women. *The Tryals of Captain John Rackam and Other Pirates*, a Jamaican pamphlet describing the court proceedings published by Robert Baldwin in 1721, contains the testimonies from Anne and Mary's trial. These documents were backed up by reports in the *American Weekly Mercury*, the *Boston Globe*, and the *Boston News-Letter*. And then there's the most famous of all pirate sources, the book from which we get basically all our modern pirate myths: Captain Charles Johnson's *A General History of the Robberies and Murders of the Most Notorious Pyrates and also their Policies, Discipline and Government from their first Rise and Settlement in the Island of Providence, in 1717, to the Present Year, 1724, with the Remarkable Actions and Adventures of the two Female Pyrates, Mary Read and Anne Bonny, to which is Prefix'd an Account of the famous Captain Avery and his Companions; with the Manner of his Death in England* (phew) from 1724. Though scholars generally view Johnson (who wrote under a pseudonym) as a fairly accurate historian, readers must consider the usual biases when reading his account of Anne and Mary. He was a British dude in the early eighteenth century, and he frames both their stories as wild romances. (They did it all for love, you see! Mary, the good heteronormative wife, and Anne, the promiscuous Irish lady!) Johnson's telling of how Anne and Mary masterfully concealed and strategically revealed their sex is also dubious, considering that trial witness Dorothy Thomas said both women were easily identifiable by their large chests. And because Johnson's book was so popular, four editions were printed in three years, with content added to jibe with what fans wanted to read. The 1726 edition includes details about Anne's first husband also being a pirate and how Anne tried to get him to sell her to Calico Jack. The 1765 edition says that, while on trial, Mary said she only got into piracy because of "Anne Bonny, who was her lover." Such pals.

But one thing Johnson's book does provide is an illustration of Anne and Mary, both dressed in jackets and trousers, brandishing swords and hatchets. They're standing on a beach surrounded by palm trees, feet planted firmly, hair flowing free. They're immortalized in this illustration as they were in life: two women pirates throwing off the expectations of the Old World, embodying the ideals of the revolutions to come. They made their own way in the world, and they did it together. And they were *pirates*. How badass is that? ✦

The Red Lanterns Shining

*THE SUPERPOWERED WARRIOR WOMEN
WHO DEFENDED CHINA*

ACTIVE CIRCA 1898–1901

Your country is being taken over. Your brothers are fighting against the invaders. And you're not allowed to leave the house. What do you do? If you're the Red Lanterns Shining of China, you call up all the toughest girls you know in the same position, run away from home, and form the most frightening, powerful, magical fighting squad your people have ever seen.

As the 1800s drew to a close, the Qing Empire, the last imperial dynasty of China, was nearing its end after more than two centuries in power. But conditions for women hadn't changed much since the dynasty kicked off in 1644. Patriarchal Confucianism, a lack of property rights, submission to fathers or husbands or even sons, confinement to the house, having babies (hopefully sons), and the extra-terrible bonus of foot binding for upper-class women (because who needs to stand or walk, anyway?) made life oppressive across the board for Qing ladies.

However, women weren't alone in facing hardship. At the turn of the century, rebellion in China was brewing in response to Western influence. Germany, Russia, France, and England occupied parts of China, and Western militaries and businesses had given way to Christian missionaries, who traveled far inland, often to villages that had never before seen a white person. They seized lands for churches, bypassed Chinese laws, and generally acted like they owned the place. The people of China were angry, and what started as stone-throwing and clock-smashing quickly turned to church-burning and foreigner-killing. The fierce anti-imperialist movement known as the Boxer Uprising had arrived. Between 1898 and 1900, the Qing court (in part afraid of the Boxers' wrath) supported the fight against a newly formed coalition of eight Western nations determined to crush them.

A rebel group of northern Chinese peasants and farm workers, the Boxers United in Righteousness were first reported early in 1898 in Guan county, about three hundred miles south of Beijing. The Boxers were independent bands of young men around 20 *sui* (years of age according to the lunar calendar), although some were as young as 12. Not necessarily particularly talented at boxing, their Western name in fact came from a series of martial-arts-type movements that the men performed before battle, which they regarded as a magic ritual that would render them invincible, particularly against bullets; after these movements, the fighters effectively fell into a trance, possessed by the spirits of powerful gods. The Boxers learned their invulnerability charms from religious leaders and market magicians, and the rituals developed in every village where the uprising spread. The Boxer magic extended beyond protection against Western weapons; it could also keep gruel pots full, teleport soldiers, and just burn things up. Fire became the Boxers' signature move; they'd draw a charm on the ground with swords or spears, invoke an enchantment, and up the Christians' buildings would go in a burst of flames. Their magic was also supposed to protect their own buildings from fire damage, though that one didn't always work out as planned. And why not?

Chicks, man! See, Boxers were not allowed to even look at women, whose *yin* (the metaphysical "feminine" side of the universe, polluted with sexual activity and childbearing) was damaging and debilitating to Boxer magic. (Personally, I feel pretty badass that my mere existence could gum up the works of an invulnerability spell, but hey.) Not surprisingly, this polluting yin meant that women were prohibited from becoming Boxers. But girls across northern China were not content to watch the world literally burn around them; many were miserable about their upcoming arranged marriages, were treated like garbage by their mothers-in-law, or were just plain trapped inside their homes with no access to the outside world. They didn't want to sit by and let the revolution happen without their help or input. Something started to stir—and the foreigners took notice. Olivia Ogren, a terrified Swedish missionary working in the China Inland Mission in Shanxi, near Beijing, wrote in June 1900 that the "long-continued drought and threatened famine" had caused whispers "that the Boxers wore buttons which kindled fires . . . and that they were stealing girls to recruit [into] the 'Red Lantern Society.'"

She almost had it right. Out of the shadows, especially in the Beijing and Tianjin areas, red lights had started to appear amid the fighting—red lights in red lanterns held by girls dressed head to toe in red, leaving fires and devastation wherever they went, if the stories were to be believed. The girls of northern China had formed their own uprising and called themselves the *Hongdeng zhao*, the Red Lantern Shining. The Red Lanterns were greatly feared but rarely seen. (Scholars take some of the oral history with a grain of salt, but the Red Lanterns *did* exist, even if who they were and what they did is somewhat, shall we say, up in the air).

Their name derives from a few places: a martial-arts organization, the Boxers' invulnerability ritual, and a religious belief that light would triumph over darkness in China when red lanterns lit up the world in rebellion. But by the spring of 1900, it pretty much universally meant a group of terrifyingly badass girls dressed entirely in red who are here to mess up the foreigners. Mostly teenage girls around "hair pin" age, or 15 years old (the hair pin symbolized entry into womanhood), the Red Lanterns were largely unmarried and premenarche (i.e., they hadn't yet gotten their periods, thanks to the drought and their diets), which meant their yin was squeaky clean. Though they rarely interacted with the Boxers, who had separate altars and training grounds, as a group they shared some similarities with their male counterparts: they organized in smaller groups, or bands; used equivalent nomenclature for their leaders (e.g., Senior Sister-Disciple and Second Sister-Disciple); trained rigorously in sword fighting and martial arts; and, of course, had magic powers.

The Red Lanterns' magic wasn't limited to setting things on fire, either. They were the most magically powerful of the rebel groups by far. They could walk on water. They could fly through the air and up to the heavens. They could attack Western ships from a distance, stop bullets in their tracks, heal the wounded, and revive the dead. If you were fighting against the Boxers and you saw red lights in the distance, you knew your end was on the horizon. (If you're skeptical, the Confucian writer Liu Dapeng noted in his *Casual Notes from Within the Garden* that, "even if they could not themselves take to flight in the sky, they mounted high walls as if they were monkeys," so one way or another, they got up there.) Best of all: the Red Lanterns could look at Chinese and Western women all they wanted, absorbing all that yin without diminishing their powers. Like the Boxers said while waiting for the Red Lanterns to arrive during the drawn-out siege of Beijing's North Cathedral: "The Red Lanterns are all girls and young women, so they do not fear dirty things."

Though they fought to preserve their native culture, the Red Lanterns largely represented the opposite of what was expected of teen girls in turn-of-the-century China. They didn't bother with traditional hair arrangements, they worked outside the home, and they definitely didn't bind their feet. According to one poem

> *The women do not comb their hair.*
> *They cut off the foreigners' heads.*
> *The women do not bind their feet.*
> *They kill all the foreigners, laughing as they go.*

Their outfits consisted of coats with tied-up sleeves, pants, hats, and shoes, plus a lantern in their right hand and a fan in their left—all in their namesake color, which was traditionally worn by new brides. With just one wave of their fans, they could set whole buildings ablaze or jump hundreds of feet into the air, returning to Earth to slice their opponents' heads off. Another poem goes

> *Wearing all red,*
> *Carrying a small red lantern,*
> *Woosh, with a wave of the fan*
> *Up they fly to heaven.*

Sometimes, they'd trade their fans for a red kerchief, a spell book, or a flower basket that caught bullets from the air.

In Shanxi, the girls venerated female deities found in popular novels at the time, like Guanyin, goddess of mercy, and Nüwa, the mother goddess. When they weren't setting things on fire, they healed wounded Boxers; cleaned, sewed, and performed other support tasks; served as lookouts; gathered intelligence; and fed hungry troops with a very Robin Hood–esque wealth distribution system (they stole grain from rich Chinese dudes and gave it to the Boxers). About once every two weeks, the Red Lanterns would walk through the streets of their villages, waving their swords as a warning. Liu Mengyang, a resident of the northern coastal city of Tianjin who wrote one of the more reliable accounts of the Red Lanterns, said that when the girls would "walk through the streets, they avoid women, who are not allowed to gaze upon them. The people all burn incense and kneel in their presence; they call them female immortals and dare not look up at them. Even the Boxer bandits, when they encounter them, fall prostrate on their knees by the side of the road." Yeah they did.

But the Red Lanterns sought to do more than impress their countrypeople. They wanted to intimidate and scare the heck out of foreigners—and by all accounts, they very much did. In July 1900, F. W. S. O'Neill, a member of the Irish Presbyterian Mission in Manchuria, wrote that the young girls of the Red Lanterns "are said to be bullet-proof. On the occasion of first attack at [Tieling], the Chinese troops were led by a maiden on horseback. She was shot in the head, and died, of course. But the story was that she became alive again." In Shanxi that same month, Friar Barnabas Nanetti da Cologna wrote that "there are women boxers called Red Lanterns, all dressed in red and carrying red lanterns everywhere. They're from eleven to fourteen years old, are unmarried, and like the young men they rage in a hypnotic sleep of evil, though even more so than the males. Based on their pagan beliefs they believe they are also invulnerable, and what is more important, they think they can fly, and destroy and burn with an invincible power." The Irish journalist George Lynch wrote in *The War of Civilisations: Being the Record of a "Foreign Devil's" Experiences with the Allies in China* that "there were societies of red lanterns, which consisted of young girls, who could walk in the air if they held a handkerchief in one hand and a red lantern in the other, which could help the Boxers to burn the missionary buildings" and that "the red lantern girls could pull down high-storied houses with thin cotton strings, and could set fire to the house simply by moving a fan, and also said that they had the power of hanging a rock of several pounds on a hair." Ai Sheng, a resident of Dingxing county, southwest of Beijing, remembered a time when the Boxers set fire to Christian homes a few months earlier in Cangju village, with the Red Lanterns in a camp nearby. "While the Red Lanterns slept in the shed," he later recalled in *The Chronological Events of the Boxer Bandits*, "their souls mounted to the clouds and called on the strange wind to help in battle." The wind fanned the flames and expedited the destruction. Supporters of the uprising would hang red lanterns on their houses to welcome the girls. "The red lantern shines," read one piece of Boxer propaganda, "lighting the path for the people."

We know of at least a few individual members of this society, the most famous of whom was the leader of the Red Lanterns in Tianjin. Born Lin Hei'er to a family that lived and worked fully on water, she spent her early years as a traveling entertainer with her father and became known for her acrobatics, opera, boxing, and whip tricks. She married another boatman and lived a fairly happy life, traveling up and down the Grand Canal between Beijing and Hangzhou until her father-in-law was imprisoned for a perceived slight against a foreigner in 1900. Committed to revenge, Lin Hei'er joined the Red Lanterns in her twenties, along with her sister-in-law, Huang Sangu, and rose quickly through the ranks when the other girls saw her martial-arts skills. She set up her home base and *Hongdeng zhao* altar on a boat in the Grand Canal, where she displayed her lanterns, decorated with red silk, satin, and a big red flag off the mast that bore her chosen name, Huanglian shengmu (Holy Mother of the Yellow Lotus).

She healed injured Boxers with water, rubbed the bodies of the dead until they came back to life, worked out battle plans with Boxer leaders, and devastated her enemies in their tracks. People treated her like a goddess. When she wasn't offering training sessions from her boat or leading battles, she acted as the personal bodyguard for the province's governor general, and in this capacity she was treated as his equal; she's said to have arrived at his house carried on a chair by four beefy dudes under a flag that read "The Protective Corps of the Holy Mother of the Yellow Lotus." (Also goals.) With that extra influence, the Yellow Lotus was able to advance the cause of the Red Lanterns, spread Boxer propaganda, and help provide food and medicine for the fighters.

Then there was Zhao Qing, a Red Lantern from Ziya, who recalled in an oral interview in the mid-1900s that her unit's Senior Sister-Disciple could fall into a deep trance in which she was capable of healing a sick person by simply clapping her hands. This 17- or 18-year-old young woman, Cui Yun Jie (Azure Cloud), had similar motivations to Yellow Lotus. An inhumanly beautiful martial-arts expert, she could leap higher than ten feet in the air and was said to have motivated the people of Beijing into staying and fighting the Westerners instead of fleeing. After she saw male Boxers commit heinous acts against female foreigners (I'm sure we can all guess what went down here), Azure Cloud invited the Boxer boys over for dinner, told them they were a disgrace, executed them as an apology to heaven, and was never seen again. Another Red Lantern around the same age arrived home after disappearing for a few days, and her parents threatened to confine her to the house. In response, she told her parents she had flown to Russia and burned down their capital city and would kill her parents if they tried to keep her inside. In Nantiancun, a 17-year-old calling herself Goddess Yang had premonitions of the Christians' next moves and stopped them in their tracks. Han Guniang, a big supporter of the aforementioned "grain redistribution," could turn a bench into a horse, a rope into a dragon, or a mat into a flying cloud. Two Red Lanterns from Baiyancun could make fire appear spontaneously.

Perhaps the most famous Red Lantern leaders were Jindao Shengmu (Holy Mother of the Golden Sword) and Lishan Laomu (Venerable Mother of the Pear Mountain), both of whom were called in during the long siege of Beijing's North Cathedral. Thousands of Christians had taken refuge in the cathedral, including adult women, which meant the Boxers found themselves at a loss after weeks of unsuccessful attempts to burn or explode the place. The women in the church were doing everything they could to disable the Boxers' powers; some accounts include references to pubic hair flags and period blood being used to ward them off (!!!). The Golden Sword arrived at the end of July 1900, and she and her Red Lanterns helped take part in the siege, counteracting the powers of the Western women's yin.

Alas, not a month later, around 20,000 troops from the Eight Nations descended on Beijing, 5,000 of which came from US President William McKinley's new base in Manila. Overwhelmed and wanting to maintain power, the Qing court decided to rewrite history a bit, withdrawing its support of the Boxers and declaring that the uprising had in fact gone against imperial wishes—and then proceeded to quash the Boxers. That's probably why you know this historical event as "the Boxer Rebellion" and not "the Boxer Uprising," though it really wasn't a rebellion against the Qing dynasty at all. The court was fully complicit.

Still, the heart of the uprising—the independence and national identity that the people of China were fighting for—lived on in tales and stories, and the empire fell to revolution just over a decade later anyway. Today it's hard to know which accounts of the Red Lanterns are reliable; there are even some references to middle-aged Blue Lanterns, elderly Black Lanterns, and shadowy White Lanterns and Green Hands. The one thing we can be sure of is that the young women of China were not happy with their circumstances or with the direction of their country, and when they had no other choices, they banded together to set their world on fire. And that's enough to set a fire in my heart, too. ✦

The Red Women of Finland

THE LEFTIST FEMALE FIGHTERS
WHO TOOK ON INEQUALITY

ACTIVE 1918–1919

Vixens. Monsters. She-wolves. Devils. The women fighting for their rights in turn-of-the-century Finland were called many things, but let's add one more name to the list, one that they'd be proud of today: social justice warriors. Allow me to explain, and I think you'll agree.

In the early 1900s, Finland was still all about that agriculture life; about 90 percent (!) of the population lived rurally, with multiple generations of women and men typically living together on farms and taking on equal, complementary amounts of work. But as industrialization spread, people started to move into cities and relationships between men and women changed rapidly; no longer led by complementary work partners, urban families became one guy who worked, one gal who stayed at home, and the kids, who were now being raised to fulfill similarly gendered roles. This new Finnish society told women they were important: They were educators of the next generation! They were responsible for raising future Finish citizens! They could, maybe, sometimes, even take on work as nurses, maids, seamstresses, or laundresses! But ultimately their place was in the home, to serve as a good example for their kids and . . . yeah, not much else.

Meanwhile, things started to get a little wild for the country at large. In 1809, Sweden had lost a war with Russia over which country had control of Finland (a conflict confusingly called the Finnish War despite Finland not actually fighting in it). Since the end of the war, the Grand Duchy of Finland had been part of the Russian Empire, and Finland was mostly chill with that because Russia granted them more autonomy than the Swedes ever had. (Also, they didn't have to pay taxes because Russia was so rich and Finland was so small that it apparently wasn't worth the hassle.) Ninety years later and one year into his reign, Nicholas II (the last emperor of Russia, aka dad of Anastasia who you may remember from the 1997 animated musical film *Anastasia*) reneged on the arrangement and took away Finland's autonomous status, deciding it was time to start in on the Russification (yes, that is a word) of Finland.

Naturally, the Finnish people, who had mostly been responsible for governing themselves for the better part of a century, took issue with this development—especially at a time when their country was going through the growing pains of industrialization (think: "my six-year-old child is being forced to work sixteen hours a day for a daily rate of one cent in a factory with no safety mechanisms, which seems bad, actually"). Maids, for example, were treated particularly poorly and often exploited in, well, probably the worst ways you can imagine. Beyond the typical workplace rights and safety issues, the working class in Finland was also denied the right to vote, which is a substantial barrier to effecting change in government. So people did what they could: band together. In 1899, the Finnish Workers Party (later the Social Democratic Party) was founded, followed by the League of Working Women a year later, who called for full suffrage for all Finnish people, regardless of class status or gender. In the fall of 1904, the women workers at the Voikkaa paper mill walked off the job when the factory refused to fire a supervisor who sexually harassed his employees. A year later, inspired by the Russian Revolution, a huge portion of the Finnish working class abandoned their posts in what became known as the Great Strike. Though it lasted only a week, the strike had a major impact on Finland's political situation; it even divided the National Guard, with some members breaking off to form the Red Guard to protect the working class.

Throughout all this fighting for social justice, the women of Finland were on the front line. Alongside the rest of the disenfranchised, they fought for their right to vote, perhaps in part because, not long before, when the country was more agrarian, they'd played a valuable and equal role in keeping their families afloat. Ten of the twenty-two members of the Great Strike's top leadership in Tampere (a city in the south of Finland) were women, and more than 200 women's suffrage meetings were held across the nation, attended by over 40,000 women. Any suggestion that the men might take the easy route and fight only for themselves was met with a clear message: do that, and the women will strike again (and stop cooking at home, too, suckers). After the Great Strike, *Palvelijatarlehti* (a periodical written by and for working women in Finland, whose name translates roughly to "The Maid's Magazine") reported that women flooded into meetings focusing on their rights and position in Finnish society, realizing "that it would depend on them whether the status of women improved or not." At a 5,000-strong rally in December 1905, the suffragettes made clear that the women of Finland refused to continue as "helpless creatures begging men for protection, but rather as their comrades in battle, free women of a free people, willing to bear all the consequences, whether they be light or heavy, that the future may weigh upon our nation's shoulders."

It worked. By the end of 1905, Russia realized its blunder and returned the country's autonomy, repealed the Russification, and even established an elected parliament. Despite previous fears of gender-segregated enfranchisement, in July 1906 Finland granted its citizens universal suffrage, becoming the first country in the *entire world* to give women the right to vote and run for office. The Red Guards were disbanded, nineteen women were elected to parliament, and everyone lived happily ever after.

Well, okay, not quite. Women now had the right to vote, but they were still expected to uphold and maintain the ideal of Finnish womanhood, marrying and staying home to educate their children. They weren't even allowed to get jobs without their husbands' permission. And the chasm between the working class and the bourgeoisie just got wider (stop me if you've heard this one before), with the majority of the people who kept the country functional receiving very little of its wealth. The Russians finally kicked Nicholas II to the curb in 1917 (sorry, Anastasia), and Finland gained full independence by December 6 of that same year. With inequality lingering and talk of revolution in the air, things didn't seem like they'd be going smoothly for much longer—and, sure enough, just over a month later, the country was embroiled in full-on civil war.

As happens in civil wars, the missions of the two factions were pretty diametrically opposed. On the right wing of the political spectrum was the White Guard, the German-backed, government-supporting conservatives who supported so-called traditional values (e.g., keeping the rich rich and the poor poor). On the left was the resurrection of the working-class Red Guard, which fought for workers' rights and the downfall of the bourgeoisie. By the end of January 1918, the Reds had control of the southern third of Finland, including its four largest cities: Helsinki, Vyborg, Turku, and Tampere. Their numbers swelled from some 40,000 in February to around 65,000 by April. The Whites, in the north, fought the encroaching Reds and the Russian soldiers remaining in the country. The Whites called it a rebellion. The Reds called it a revolution.

And since Finnish women are not the type to sit by quietly while their country goes to heck in a handbasket, the ladies were active on both sides of the dispute. For the White women, their roles were constrained to what society had decided were proper, ladylike wartime duties, such as nursing, cooking, sewing, and "arousing patriarchal spirit," whatever that means. They weren't paid. They weren't soldiers. They were the mothers and wives of Finland, and they were meant to take care of the men.

Which is probably why the bourgeoisie was downright scandalized by the brash, nonconformist women of the Red Guard. Taking inspiration from the Women's Battalions of the Russian Revolution, Finnish ladies joined the Red Guard in droves—not only because of their ideology, but also because the Reds ran newspaper advertisements for positions that paid twice what women were making in households or factories; eventually they even paid the women in groceries. In a country suffering from unemployment and food-supply crises, that was a pretty big deal. Thousands of Red women joined the cause, at first taking on roles similar to their White counterparts: maintenance, provisions, accommodations, nursing, working in confiscated factories, and preparing equipment. Priority for prime support roles was given to older and married women, leaving plenty of Red women, many as young as 14, looking for ways to contribute. For them, that meant picking up a gun and killing some rich folks.

Whether society liked it or not, Red women initially guarded strategic locations (to free up men for fighting); then, as the war continued and they received training, they made their way to the front lines. Across the south of Finland, women's units took shape. Fifteen- to 20-year-old women joined up, almost always with a friend at their side—for them, the fight for their rights was an adventure to be shared with their closest buds from their workplaces or social lives. In short, the Red women were in this, and they were in this together. They were a force not even the men's Red Guard was prepared to deal with; though Red leadership had declared at the beginning of March 1918 that women should stick to support roles, by the end of the month they agreed to let the existing women's units contribute on the battlefield. As for the Red women, they were excited to be doing what they felt was the real work of the war: "They founded a women's guard here, and anyhow I'm such an enthusiastic person so of course I went there first," wrote Sally Rosendahl, one of the first of the 166 front-line volunteers from Tampere, in a letter on March 15. "You can't believe how enthusiastic I was about going to the front. Now I am going back on watch at eight although I just came off duty."

Sure, this gal and her friends were excited because they were fighting for their civil rights, but also they got to wear *pants*. Red women threw off the constraints of traditional Finnish women's expected behavior, which included ditching their dresses and skirts for trousers and men's uniforms and cutting their hair. Nobel Prize–nominated author and journalist Juhani Aho described the first Red woman soldier he ever saw as "a chubby little woman, fat and plump, a rifle on her shoulder, an ammunition belt on her waist, a yellow laced shoe on her feet, a woolen knitted skiing cap on her head—in short a woman in arms." In his memoirs, the German commander Rüdiger von der Goltz remembered "women wearing pants in the first row, lots of Russian uniforms"; he further noted that "hardly have the French attacked as fiercely as did these fanatical defenders of the new canon of barbarity." After the war, witnesses in court recalled seeing 15-year-old Laura Alanen of the Red Guard "riding a horse[,] dressed in menswear and her hair loose, in front of the cortege," a sight that stayed with them for months.

By April 1918, more than 2,000 women were front-line combatants in the Red Guard. In a 1920 book about the effects of war on young people, the educator and former parliament member Vilho Reima wrote that he'd hear Red women saying, "'all the bourgeoisie people must be killed. And if the men can't do it, we women will go. We will do like they did in Tampere. We will take the guns and swords in our hand and we will clean it up.'" He could have been referring to women like "the famous Red Amazon" and "killing angel" Toini Mäkelä, the 23-year-old leader of the 150 women in guard work, intelligence, and battle at Vyborg. But Vilho was probably referring to the women at Pispala, a neighborhood in Tampere, who were said to keep fighting long after the men had surrendered in a battle. "The men proposed retreating, but the women said they had come to fight and they did not retreat," the Social Democrat Jukka Lehtosaari recalled in a 1929 memoir. "They pushed on with the attack, towards certain death. The butchers withdrew. The women soldiers bore the glory for many victories. When the men's courage had failed already, the women persisted with the attack or held their positions." Girls as young as 14 and 15 were part of that Pispala women's unit, under the command of 18-year-old Emma Oksala. They may have been young, but they were tough as nails.

So the Whites not only had to suffer the perceived indignity of meeting their former male employees on an equal playing field, but they also had to come face-to-face on the battlefield with their former female housemaids, servants, and governesses. Women were supposed to be the givers and caretakers of life, the epitome of femininity; but the Red women were brutal killers, masculine dressers, and determined destroyers of the status quo. The Whites hated the Reds in general, but they found the Red women especially reprehensible, seeing these "vixens with malicious tongues" as monstrous and using them in propaganda against the Social Democrats across the nation. An article published by the newspaper *Aamulehti* in April 1918 read in part: "If a real red guardsman villain is called a human beast, this name is too lenient to his feminine counterpart." That same month, a writer for *Newspaper Ilkka* declared that the women soldiers' combination of menswear and heavy makeup made them look like "little devils." White propagandists split the Red women into four shame-worthy categories: women soldiers, or "tigresses"; mothers, the "sources of evil"; nurses, "sisters of love"; and girlfriends of Russian soldiers, the "Russian brides." The Finnish newspaper *Keskisuomalainen* compared Red women to she-wolves (*awooo!*) who needed to be put down before they could make and educate more little Red wolves. It was said that Red women even baked guns into the bread they delivered to their husbands in prison.

Now, I'd love to be able to tell you that the Reds trounced some rich butt and sent the country into a revolution that uplifted the working class and crops flourished and they made seventeen female superhero movies about it, but, unfortunately, this civil war didn't turn out that way. The White Guard had a conscripted national Finnish army, the German army, and a bunch of money working for it. The Red Guard was unprepared and understaffed, and Russia was in no hurry to support it; they thought the Reds weren't serious about revolution and were also trying to negotiate a shaky peace with Germany after their conflict in World War I. The civil war lasted only three and a half months, from late January to the middle of May 1918, but more than 36,000 people died, most of them Reds. To put that into perspective, that's about one percent of the entire population of Finland at the time. In May, the Whites took control of the country, and tens of thousands of Reds were prosecuted for treason, including 5,000 Red women (even the nurses who feigned thinking that they had joined the Red Cross). More than 400 Red women were shot, and over 100 others died of hunger in prison camps. Many had their children "re-educated," and others were forced to flee to Russia or America to escape persecution. Equally as tragic, the Whites reversed the enfranchisement laws the Reds had fought for, stripping anyone who had even the vaguest connection to the Reds of their full citizenship. Without the power to vote, run for office, get good jobs, or exercise freedom of assembly or the press, the working classes were silenced and sidelined once again.

But the Red women's efforts weren't in vain. In spite of the Whites' attempts to render them powerless, the Social Democrats won 40 percent of the seats in parliament in the 1919 elections, thanks in part to a historic turnout from women at the polls; 70 percent of Finnish women voted. In the years after the war, Finland established compulsory education, loosened land-ownership rights so more people had the chance to own (not just work) land, restored freedom of association so that unions and social groups could organize again, guaranteed freedom of religion, and, by 1920, fully pardoned nearly 40,000 Reds, restoring their citizenship. Nevertheless, Red widows (both the widows of Red insurgents and former Red women) were denied war pensions until the 1940s, and most Reds resisted sharing their side of the story for another two decades after that. Today, however, scholars like Tiina Lintunen are working hard to rediscover the fascinating lives of the Red women, and institutions are spotlighting this period of Finnish history. The Vapriikki Museum has a permanent exhibit dedicated to Tampere in 1918, complete with sleds, clothes, and letters, and Werstas, the Finnish labor museum, recently ran an exhibition on the women of the Red Guard. And though historians still debate how to classify the uprising, for the Red women of the war—women who defied all expectation and social norms to fight for their civil rights—there's no doubt it was a revolution. And, ultimately, they won. ✦

CHAPTER 4

SCIENTIST SQUADS

Women have had to fight for every right they've been granted—even the right to fight for their own education. First taking on incredible odds even to get through the doors at universities, women have had to contend with everything from being unfairly treated by male doctors and excluded from laboratories to having their names erased from the historical record of their contributions. Let's meet science history's toughest groups of gal pals.

Anandibai Joshi, Sabat Islambooly, and Kei Okami

THE FIRST EASTERN DOCTORS OF WESTERN MEDICINE

ACTIVE 19TH CENTURY

One of the world's best historical photographs looks almost too incredible to be real the first time you see it. The black-and-white image shows two women seated, with a third standing between them, and it's dated October 10, 1885. On the left, a small Indian woman wearing a sari smiles into the camera. Text on the photo identifies her as "Dr. Anandabai Joshee" from "Seranysore, India." On the right sits "Dr. Tabat M. Islambooly" of "Damascus, Syria" with a harp resting against her lap, her serious-looking face framed by coins descending from her headdress. Between them, a Japanese woman from "Tokio" with an impish look determinedly stares away from the camera, an obi tied tightly around her ki-mono, haori on top. This photograph has languished for over a century in the archives of the medical school attended by these three women doctors from Asia—three friends, far from home, who bonded over their shared passion and path.

No two patriarchal cultures have developed exactly the same way, but many of them maintain the dudes-in-charge status quo by limiting, or preventing entirely, educational opportunities for women. Although men have traditionally been free to study sci-ence, medicine, and math, women's learning has in many cases been confined to domestic arts like housekeeping, playing in-struments, needlework, weaving, and cooking. Until the mid-nineteenth century, no modern institutions of higher learning admitted women. There are obviously many reasons why this was a bad thing, but one of the most globally and directly harmful was that, for a very long time, there were no women doctors.

Though women have long tended to one another's health as apothecaries and empirics (a kind of general practitioner who specialized in reproductive health and hands-on healing), they were always marginalized and never considered "true" doctors. For example, in medieval Europe, laws limited the practice of medicine to people who were licensed through universities—that is, Christian males—and fined, jailed, or exiled any woman who practiced anyway. To make matters worse, the "doctoring" that these universities taught was entirely theoretical and involved a lot of reading of Galen and Plato and not a lot of surgery or pre-scription writing or even talking to actual patients. That, coupled with the shame women were taught to feel about their "sinful" bodies, a theme common in many religions the world over, meant that most women would literally rather die than suffer the embarrassment of asking for medical help.

Even as medical school curricula became more evidence-based and driven by scientific discovery instead of superstition (and therefore somewhat effective at teaching medicine), women were still excluded from attending. It wasn't until 1847 that Elizabeth Blackwell busted barriers and became the first American woman to attend medical school. Three years later, a group of abolitionist and pro-women's-movement Quakers founded the Female Medical College of Pennsylvania, a school with a groundbreaking mission: not only did it educate and graduate some of the world's first female doctors of modern Western medicine, but it also sent students to provide outpatient services to the most vulnerable and marginalized residents of Philadelphia, including immigrant and Black women, at a time when discrimination was rampant.

This outreach was no coincidence, and it wasn't just for patients, either. The school was also one of the most inclusive and encouraging of diverse candidates of any institution of higher learning in the world. In 1852, thirteen years before the abolition of slavery, the college admitted a Black woman in her late forties, Sarah Mapps Douglass, to its third session. (Though she didn't graduate, Sarah went on to teach courses for Black women in medicine.) Rebecca Cole, the second Black woman to earn an MD in the United States, graduated from the school (by then renamed the Women's Medical College of Pennsylvania, or WMCP) in 1867 and joined Elizabeth Blackwell's hospital for women as a resident physician.

The WMCP focused particularly on obstetrics, gynecology, and preventative medicine—specialties often neglected by mainstream medical schools. As time passed and women beyond US borders began to learn of the school's success graduating women doctors (and treating women patients), interest began to grow. And the school's dean—Rachel Bodley—was ready for it. Heading up the institution from 1874 until her death in 1886, Dean Rachel was dedicated to recruiting women from across the globe to become doctors, in the hopes that they'd be able to return to their countries to assist the women they knew needed their help—the very women who had inspired them to travel to a foreign, and potentially unfriendly, country for an education.

Which brings us back to the amazing moment that Kate Hurd-Mead, a member of WMCP class of 1888, remembered as beginning with an invitation from the dean that read: "Ladies, you are invited to a reception . . . at my home to meet Ramabai, wisest of Indian women, and Mrs. Okami, your classmate, a pioneer from far Japan, and Mrs. Joshee, . . . and Susan Le Flesche, another of our students, a full-blooded American Indian from the great plains, and Sabat Islambooly, a Syrian from Damascus." From this reception comes that remarkable 1885 photograph of Anandi, Sabat, and Kei, three women who relied on their mutual friendship and singular understanding during a difficult but exciting time in their lives.

Each of these three women had a difficult and distinct path to that reception at the dean's home. Thanks to her letters preserved in the WMCP archives and an 1888 biography written by the feminist Caroline Healey Dall (which includes a foreword by Rachel Bodley), the woman we know most about is Anandi Joshi. Born in 1865 as Yamuna in the city of Kalyan, her greatest wish was for an education—a big ask for an Indian girl at a time when women weren't even allowed to read or write. It was her tutor Gopalrao—whom she married at the age of 9—who gave her the name Anandibai, which means "joy of my heart."

Anandi's purpose in life crystallized in her early teens when she and Gopal lost an infant son at just ten days old. She believed his life could've been saved had she been able to get him to a proper doctor—so she decided she would become a doctor herself. Of course, this wasn't going to be easy: schools and hospitals in India were openly hostile to women who sought an education, and Anandi's walk to classes was punctuated by thrown rocks, screamed obscenities, and spit (not to mention the discrimination she and Gopal already faced as two of the few Maharashtra Hindus in Serampore). Frustrated by their circumstances and by the lack of opportunity for his wife in India, Gopal wrote to American Presbyterian missionaries in the hopes that they would sponsor his wife to study medicine abroad. The missionaries forwarded Gopal's letter to Royal Wilder, the editor of the *Missionary Review*, who published his response in the journal. Essentially, Royal wrote that Anandi was more than welcome to study at one of the mission schools in India, so long as she just went ahead and renounced her Hinduism and became a Christian. (Very accepting of them!)

Luckily, halfway across the globe, another woman was about to become Anandi's best friend. Theodicia Carpenter of Roselle,

New Jersey, had picked up a copy of the *Missionary Review* while waiting for a dentist appointment. Finding Wilder's response to Gopal's letter pretty un-Christian, Theodicia copied the address Gopal had provided and, after her teeth were clean and she was sent home with a new toothbrush (that was probably a thing back then, too, right?), wrote to Anandi in 1880. Theodicia told Anandi she was welcome in her home anytime.

That first letter was the beginning of an incredibly strong long-distance friendship between Anandi and Theodicia, with the two of them exchanging information on everything from their daily lives and their cultures to their problems and their dreams. They sent each other newspapers, magazines, pictures, flowers, seeds, even hair clippings (though Anandi pointed out that, in her culture, only widows were allowed to cut their hair). Theodicia, who was particularly fascinated by Anandi's nose ring, called the friendship "a regular course of education in Hindu manners, customs, religious rites, and everything of interest." Anandi made it clear to Theodicia that she had it easy compared to women in India: "Your American widows may have difficulties and inconveniences to struggle with, but weighed in the scale against ours, all of them put together are but as a particle against a mountain." Theodicia often sent medicine when Anandi was ill and always maintained that open invitation to her home. But Anandi—a Brahmin woman who wasn't supposed to travel overseas in the first place—just didn't have the cash to afford the trip.

So in February 1883, without any prepared notes, 18-year-old Anandi marched into the Serampore College Hall and gave a speech to the town (she was the first woman ever to do so). "In my humble opinion there is a growing need for Hindu lady doctors in India," she said, "and I volunteer to qualify myself for one." Anandi explained that she'd travel alone to America to get the education she couldn't in her home country, maintaining her Hindu customs the whole time, and would return to use her knowledge to benefit the women of India. "I will go as a Hindu," Anandi said, "and come back here to live as a Hindu." Her speech was so impressive that the post office director general set up an education fund for Anandi, raising enough for a single ticket on a steamer ship.

And so, on June 4, 1883, Anandi Joshi arrived in New York, making her the first Hindu woman to set foot in America. She and Theodicia sent word to the WMCP about her circumstance, with Anandi requesting admission so that she might be able to "render to my poor suffering country women the true medical aid they so sadly stand in need of, and which they would rather die for than accept at the hand of a male physician." Their appeal worked. Dean Rachel admitted Anandi with a start date of October 3, granted her a scholarship to cover the $325.50 tuition, and even gave the new student a place to live in her own house. Anandi— whom Rachel would later call a "brave little pioneer" with a "beautiful life"—finished her four-year medical degree in just three and graduated from the WMCP in 1886, with her husband, Gopal, in the crowd. Her thesis, "Obstetrics among the Aryan Hindoos," was the longest of anyone in her class and was even read by Queen Victoria herself (Rachel sent her a copy, which a royal secretary reported the Queen read "with much interest").

It was during her time at the WMCP that Anandi met her

two doctor friends, Sabat Islambooly (whose name is misspelled in the photograph) and Kei Okami. Sadly, we know very little about Sabat, in part because nobody in the West could figure the young Syrian woman's name. (American newspapers at the time refer to her as Sabat K. Selemphooly and Sabat M. Selamhooly, and current records identify her as Tabat Islambouly, Tabat Istanbuli, and Thabat Islambooly, among others. All official WMCP records—aside from the photograph typo—give her name as Sabat M. Islambooly.)

We can be certain that Sabat matriculated in the 1885–86 school year, around the time Anandi was preparing to graduate. Like Anandi, Sabat would have taken courses in chemistry and toxicology, anatomy, physiology and hygiene, general pathology, obstetrics, diseases of women and children, and more. She briefly left the institution (possibly due to illness) but was readmitted, and she graduated on March 13, 1890, receiving her doctorate of medicine from the school's president T. Morris Perot. Sabat returned to the Middle East, and an alumnae census taken in 1919 placed her in Cairo, Egypt. That was the last time the WMCP had contact with her; searches for the doctor continued well into the 1950s but turned up nothing. Her name appeared on a list of "lost alumnae" in 1926, one of the few with a black ink slash next to it that, given a similar handwritten note farther down the page, may indicate that the searcher had determined she'd passed away.

But in 2010, Najeeb Jarrar and his marketing team at Google Middle East and North Africa managed to confirm new details about Sabat's life. They found that she was the daughter of a rich merchant from a notable family with both Muslim and Jewish members in Damascus's Jewish Quarter. A few years after her return to Syria Sabat did move to Egypt with her entire family; she had a permit from the authorities in Cairo to practice medicine as of 1936. Turns out information about the Islamboly/Istanboly family is so scarce because some of Sabat's relatives were involved in the "Damascus affair" of 1840, in which thirteen prominent Jewish community members were accused of the ritualistic murder of a French Christian monk, prompting many family members to change their names and destroy records connecting them to those accused of wrongdoing. We may never learn more details about Sabat's life, but even from the little we know, we can tell she worked hard to make her dreams happen.

Rounding out the trio of barrier-breaking lady doctors was Kei Okami. Kei was born Nishida Keiko in northern Japan's Aomori prefecture in 1859. Though she was eager for an education, Kei didn't have a ton of options; her best bet was to be baptized and attend Christian schools, so that's the direction she went. At the American Mission Home, missionaries like Mrs. Maria T. True (a teacher who would become Kei's lifelong friend and coworker) taught Kei to speak English, read the Bible, and practice Western customs like eating with a knife and fork. Kei graduated at 19 and taught English for the next several years at another missionary institution, Sakurai Girls' School (where Mrs. True became principal in 1887), before realizing that, really, the best way she could help other women in Japan was to become a doctor. But Kei found herself again facing a challenge: the woman who would become Japan's first lady doctor, Ginko Ogino, had just started to petition the government for the right to take the medical exams but was being consistently rebuffed. The only way to skip the Japanese examinations was to earn one's license abroad. At age 25, in a love match of which her father did not approve, Kei married Senkichirō Okami, an art teacher at Shoei Girls' School, the founder of a Christian school, and a graduate of the Imperial College of Engineering's art department, a month before he was transferred to a technical school in Michigan in 1884. Seeing her chance to travel and finally get her medical education, Kei went for it and followed Senkichirō to the United States that December.

Thanks to Dean Rachel's admission and financial aid from the Woman's Foreign Missionary Societies of the Presbyterian Church (in their bulletin Kei was described as "a rare little woman," "timid," and "sensitive"), Kei was able to attend the WMCP, living hundreds of miles away from her husband. There, Kei would meet and befriend Anandi, Sabat, and another noteworthy woman in her year, Susan La Flesche Picotte, the first Native American woman to receive an MD from an American medical institution (and who also described Kei as "very small and pretty," aww). In addition to her studies, Kei wrote about her culture and background: in a piece titled "Japanese Costume," published in a children's magazine in 1888, she educated young American children about traditional Japanese clothing. Kei's English writing reveals her wickedly wry sense of humor; she described kimono like this: "They are very loose all over, and opened in the front from the waist to the hem of the skirt. They are secured or fastened simply by overlapping the edges together in front, and kept in place by tying a string around the body. Thus it is quite imaginable that one had to be very cautious out in a windy day in this dress." Reflecting on the coldest winter she'd experienced in Tokyo, in which the temperature dropped to just 23 degrees Fahrenheit, Kei also wrote that, though snow and ice were "the usual accompaniments of our winter season" in Japan, the wintry conditions were not at all "as they are here in Philadelphia as to the quantity and frequency."

Upon her graduation on March 14, 1889, Kei became the first Japanese woman to receive a degree in Western medicine from a Western institution. The Chinese diplomat Wu Tingfang spoke at Kei's commencement ceremony and derided American men who looked down on WMCP graduates, saying that he was "not a little surprised to learn that for all the boast of Anglo-Saxon fairness and chivalry, medical women have had a hard time in fighting their way against strong opposition at every step to public recognition and professional standing." Give it to 'em straight, man.

It's not that difficult to imagine that Sabat, Anandi, and Kei bonded at WCMP over their shared circumstances: being Asian women in an unfamiliar country, learning medicine not in their native language in order to serve the women of their beloved homelands. But we don't need to make this up; we know that they were friends because of one of Anandi's letters to Theodicia, in which she recounts the day of her final medical exam:

"Results received yesterday and I am passed. I am thankful, for my patience was almost worn out. On the last question of the last paper I broke down, and could not even see whether I finished my sentence. I pinned the papers together and left the room without even bowing to the Professor. Our Japanese friend did very well. The Syrian student, after most wonderful and formidable attacks of diseases and rewarding her benefactors and well-wishers with her ingratitude, was made to leave us. Her condition is sadder than death, if death is at all sad. She brought tears of pity to my eyes,—eyes that had so far had no occasion to shed tears of such pity or disgust. We were all miserable on her account."

Such deep feeling for Sabat, plus an outright admission of friendship for Kei, is exactly what you might expect from Anandi, and there's no doubt the three girls helped one another through challenging times during those dark, studious Philadelphia winters. With support from Susan and Rachel and Theodicia, all three women would go on to become the first women from their respective countries to earn their medical degrees in the West.

A month after graduation, with her foreign license in hand, Kei boarded a ship in San Francisco with her husband and returned to Japan to serve her countrywomen, an act her benefactors called "akin to heroism." Kei was offered a dream job as the brand-new position of head of gynecology (formally known as the "Superintendent of the Female Department") at Tokyo's Jikei Hospital, where she worked for two years. When Empress Shōken, a financial supporter of the hospital, visited in 1892, her husband, Emperor Meiji, forbade Kei (and no other doctors but Kei) from attending the imperial audience because of her gender. Kei resigned her post in disgust (like, what's a girl gotta do for some respect, here?), an act that one contemporary Japanese source described as almost as serious as *seppuku,* the ritual suicide of earlier generations.

Nonetheless, things worked out all right for Kei. She started her own medical practice out of her home, and served on the Japanese arm of the missionary Philadelphia Committee, which provided scholarships for students to pursue English education at an American school. She reunited with her former teacher and mentor, Mrs. True, and together they worked to establish an *eisei-en* (a sanitarium, sometimes called *Kouseien*) in 1897 in Tokyo. This thirteen-bed branch of the Akasaka Hospital operated for nine years as a long-term care home and prevention center for women with tuberculosis, as well as a nursing school for women studying under Mrs. True's supervision. By running her clinic and briefly returning to teaching English, Kei helped Japanese women until she was diagnosed with breast cancer in 1908, the same year she lost her oldest daughter Meray to cancer at just 23 years old. Kei transitioned into a well-earned retirement, caring for her two sons and volunteering for missionary organizations. In 1939, just before the start of World War II, a WMCP representative traveled to Japan to photograph the then-legendary Kei at her home. In 1941, five years after her husband's death, Kei passed away at the age of 82.

As for Sabat, although the folks at Google weren't able to find her exact birth or death dates, they know that her cousin's house is still standing today and that a distant great-grandson of one of her cousins currently lives in Canada. Sabat likely treated women in Cairo until her death, possibly around 1941.

Anandi, who'd struggled with illness even before leaving India for medical school, turned down an opportunity to travel to America and an internship at the New England Hospital for

Women and Children because of her poor health. Instead, she sailed back to India in October 1886 and took a position as physician in charge of the female ward at Albert Edward Hospital in the southwestern city of Kolhapur, where she also intended to direct a new program for training girls as general practitioners. Sadly, it was not to be; Anandi passed away from tuberculosis in her mother's arms three months after returning to her homeland. Her obituary praised her for proving that "the great qualities—perseverance, unselfishness, undaunted courage and an eager desire to serve one's country—do exist in the so-called weaker sex." Anandi's ashes were buried in Theodicia's family cemetery in Poughkeepsie, New York—pals to the very end.

Inspired by Anandi, Kei, and Sabat's success, Dean Rachel Bodley and her successor, Clara Marshall, continued to admit women from around the world. In 1904, the WMCP announced that it had "graduated pupils from more than forty States and Territories of this country, and from Canada, Prince Edward Island, Nova Scotia, New Brunswick, Jamaica, Brazil, England, Sweden, Denmark, Switzerland, Russia, Syria, India, China, Japan, Burmah, Australia and the Congo Free State"—none of which would have been possible without those first three women and the support of the ladies who believed in them. Though Anandi, Kei, and Sabat followed different paths to different places, their friendship—and the photograph that captured it—changed not only their lives and the lives of their many patients, but also the practice of medicine the world over. And that is absolutely, 100 percent true. ✦

The Edinburgh Seven

THE FIRST WOMEN MEDICAL STUDENTS IN GREAT BRITAIN

ACTIVE 19TH CENTURY

Sophia Jex-Blake. Isabel Thorne. Edith Pechey. Matilda Chaplin. Helen Evans. Mary Anderson. Emily Bovell. You might not have heard these seven names before, but if you've ever been grateful for your ability to be treated by a woman doctor who might actually understand your problems and take you seriously, these are the gals who get you and then some. Meet the first women ever to attend medical school in Great Britain.

In the previous profile (see page 152), we learned about international students like Anandi and Sabat flocking to America in the late nineteenth century to earn their medical degrees. But why not to Britain? For one thing, breaking from tradition was a fairly American notion; in England, tradition is what created the Great British Empire, responsible for All Civilization (in their extremely biased opinion, anyway). Secondly, there was a logistical problem—well, okay, several logistical problems, all stemming from the Medical Act of 1858. In an attempt to unify Britain's medical field and to prevent the proliferation of quacks and ineffective (and/or dangerous) patent medicine, the British Parliament declared that you could only be a real doctor if you passed the qualifying exams at one of nineteen accredited institutions, and only if you'd taken the requisite courses needed to pass at said institutions. Institutions that, of course, had never accepted a woman medical student.

Until, that is, Sophia Jex-Blake arrived on the scene. Bright, opinionated, and strong-minded from the day she was born in 1840 in Hastings, England, young Sophia was sent to boarding school by her relatively privileged family in an effort to mitigate what teachers called her "wilful [*sic*], insubordinate, often regrettably unladylike" personality. It didn't work, obviously; one of her schoolmates remembered her as "very passionate but very penitent afterwards." Sophia went on to study at Queen's College in London and accepted a job as a math tutor, earning one hundred pounds per year until 1861. Her father, who already supplied her with twice as much annually, was appalled, telling Sophia that a working woman was degrading herself. (Sophia wondered why her brother could earn a salary and she couldn't. Her father's answer: because Tom was a man, of course. Naturally, Sophia took the job *and* the salary.)

After a brief stint teaching in Germany in 1862, 25-year-old Sophia found herself thinking about opening a college for women in her home country. An inspiring 1865 visit to America and a close relationship with the British social reformer Octavia Hill (so close Sophia "I love women too much ever to love a man" Jex-Blake even moved in with Octavia and wrote about kissing her—gal pals!) solidified Sophia's desire to improve the prospects available to middle-class women in the United Kingdom. And not as second-class citizens, either; Sophia wanted women to be able to attend the same schools with the same teachers and take the same exams as men, no exceptions. Knowing England was always going to be a tough place to enact change, Sophia set her sights on Scotland, where the Edinburgh Ladies' Education Association had been working hard on making lectures available to women—not necessarily with an eye to employment, but it was a good first step.

With encouragement from some of the school's senior staff, in March 1869 Sophia scored permission from the University of Edinburgh to attend a natural history and botany class (with lots of addendums and caveats, etc.). But a month later the university court upheld an appeal against Sophia, ruling that there were too many "difficulties at present standing in the way of carrying out the resolution of the Senatus, as a temporary arrangement in the interest of one lady."

Well then, Sophia must have thought. *I guess I'll just have to come back with more ladies.*

Fortunately, the media gave her a boost. The *Scotsman*, a national newspaper edited by Alexander Russel (a supporter of the women's rights movement), reported dutifully and in full on the events of Sophia's admission to and quick expulsion from classes at Edinburgh University, and, before long, papers across the UK were picking up the story. Sophia started to receive letters of support, the first of which came from Isabel Thorne, a 35-year-old mother of four. Married to a tea merchant, Isabel had lived for just over a decade in Shanghai, where one of her children died tragically due to lack of proper medical care, and where she'd seen firsthand that women outside the UK needed help from women doctors as well. Following her time in China, Isabel had begun training in London at Queen's College and at the Ladies' Medical College, a short-lived institution for midwives that was opened in 1864 by the Female Medical Society as a way to kind of circumvent the Medical Act. (Midwifery was unregulated by the law, but instruction was limited and woefully inadequate.) After a year of such restricted training, Isabel wrote to Sophia: "I should be glad, if you renew your application [to the Faculty of Medicine], to join you in doing so, and I believe I know two or three other ladies who would be willing to do the same." By July 9, Sophia had already asked Isabel if she would matriculate with her in the fall.

Next came a letter from Edith Pechey, an apprentice to Elizabeth Garrett, England's only registered woman doctor (via a since-closed Society of Apothecaries loophole in which anyone registered as an official apothecary was also automatically listed on the national medical register). In her letter, Edith asked Sophia, with truly charming modesty, "Do you think anything more is requisite to ensure success than moderate abilities and a good share of perseverance? I believe I may lay claim to these, together with a real love of the subject of study." Sophia was considerably more effusive upon meeting 24-year-old Edith, writing in her journal that Edith was "strong, ready-handed, with 'faculty,' great ability, resolution, judgment; great calmness and quiet of manner and action, and probably strength of feeling; good taste, good manner; very pleasant face; rather good feet and hands; considerable sense of humor; lots of energy and interest in things, — witness dissecting the slugs, keeping caterpillars, etc. In fine, as good an ally and companion as could well be had." (People just don't compliment their friends' hands and feet enough these days, you know?) Sophia found her two new friends amenable to her ultimate goals, writing: "Mrs. Thorne and Miss Pechey agreed with me that we must find a way in which women could enter the medical profession in Great Britain, and in compliance with British law."

And there were more to come. (We're trying to get to seven, remember?) Matilda Chaplin, another Ladies' Medical College student around the same age as Edith, was next to join the group. Sophia met with another supporter for a late dinner (at 10 p.m., which Sophia—understandably—complained about), a widow with "clear good eyes and face" and a penchant for botany. Sophia found her to be "a *very* nice woman of thirty-three or thirty-four with curiously white hair,—Mrs. [Helen] Evans, I think. She and I held together on almost all subjects. She would like to study Medicine (and I am sure has the power)." Sophia welcomed her to the circle—and also became Helen's math tutor.

On October 19, 1869, Sophia, Isabel, Edith, Matilda, and Helen took the matriculation exam at the University of Edinburgh, and all passed with above-average grades (well, except for one close call in math, but we've all been there). This feat caused opponents of their "so-called experiment" to realize, as Sophia put it, "that if it was to be suppressed at all, vigorous measures must be taken for that purpose." With that, they became the first women to enroll at a UK university, starting classes at the University of Edinburgh's Faculty of Medicine. "Won after all!" wrote Sophia, "and I do think this must be at last 'the beginning of the end.'" Shortly after, this little gang was rounded out by 32-year-old Mary Anderson (soon to be Elizabeth Garrett's sister-in-law), and 28-year-old Emily Bovell, who was following in the footsteps of her grandfather who worked as a doctor in Barbados. Together, these women became known as the Edinburgh Seven, or, as Sophia sometimes called them, the *Septum Contra Edinam*: the "Seven Against Edinburgh."

Their nickname wasn't just for funsies, either. Acceptance to the university was only the start of the group's journey, and in the next two years the women faced protest, drama, controversy, and, of course, examinations. Male students harassed the Seven constantly, shouting obscenities like "Whore!" at them and following them down school hallways and in public. The women had their doorbell and nameplates damaged; fireworks strapped to their door; smoke blown in their faces; disgusting letters left for them to read; and lecture-hall doors slammed in their faces amid wolf whistles and howls. The unsympathetic university (stop me if you've heard this one before) just shrugged and said the administration had no control over what students did outside the classroom. But it wasn't just students; much of this nasty behavior was incited by two professors, Thomas Laycock, who thought women who wanted to be doctors were probably secret prostitutes, and Robert Christison, a longtime widow, father of three sons, man with no sisters, former royal physician, and grade-A sexist.

The Seven also struggled to find instructors. According to Sophia, "certain all-powerful members of the College of Physicians and Surgeons had resolved to ostracise any medical man who agreed to give us instructions." Even the women's fees to attend the school were more than twice what male students paid because they had to take entirely separate classes (mixed-gender classes were a big no-no at that time). Luckily, Sophia was able to cover their fees, and the women found a sort of home base in the residence Sophia and Edith shared. Despite all their hardships, at least the Seven, in their fearsome formation, were getting a true medical education, exactly in line with the male students.

Or so they thought. When Edith ranked third in a chemistry class of three hundred (and first among those taking chemistry for the first time), she qualified for the Hope Scholarship, an award that waived lab fees for the top four chemistry students each year. But her professor (and otherwise stuffy white dude) Crum Brown denied Edith the scholarship, arguing that she was not technically a "member of the class" because the women were taught separately from the men. The Seven appealed the decision, which was especially ironic because, as Sophia pointed out, the prize had "been founded by the late Professor Hope from the proceeds of lectures given to ladies some fifty years earlier." The university decided from then on to grant the Seven the same records of attendance as male students (guaranteeing their ability to take their final exams), but nevertheless refused to grant Edith the scholarship.

The Seven did have some support from dudes, however: notably, English professor David Masson, writer Charles Reade (who fictionalized their struggle in a book called *A Woman-Hater*), and *Scotsman* editor Alexander Russel (who later married one of the Seven and became Mr. Helen Evans). They also won the sympathy of the wider press, including the *British Medical Journal* and London's *Times* and *Spectator*. But the people who truly mattered—the medical gatekeepers at the university—remained very much against the idea of women becoming doctors.

As you may have guessed, some opposition to the Seven came from a place of pure, unadulterated misogyny. Male doctors were sure that the female brain was biologically smaller than men's and therefore incapable of higher intelligence. One such doctor, Henry Maudsley, famously wrote that any woman who engaged in too much "laborious" thinking would render herself incapable of pregnancy. Another, Dr. Henry Bennett, trotted out the ol' lady-hatin' and racist chestnut "Well, if women are so great, why have white men been responsible for all science?" He wrote: "I know of no great discovery changing the surface of science that owes its existence to a woman of our or of any race"—a statement that conveniently ignores the fact that women were literally kept out of universities. Beyond the run-of-the-mill women-hating, male doctors were also worried about losing female patients once these newly minted hypothetical future women doctors arrived on the scene. As one Scottish physician put it in the *Boston Medical and Surgical Journal*: "An' when the leddies get degrees, / Depen' upon't there's nocht'll please / Till they hae got oor chairs an' fees, / An there's an end o' you an' me."

Regardless of where it came from, the anger just kept growing. It finally came to a head in 1870, when the Seven petitioned the Royal Infirmary to attend classes with their male colleagues so that they could properly qualify for graduation. Furious, their dude classmates created a counterpetition, complaining that if mixed-gender classes were allowed, they would have to edit their curriculum and discussions to account for the women's fragility. (They also argued that the presence of female students would be distracting and tempting, which sounds like a case of "that's your problem," but, you know, whatever.) In the span of just seven hours, 504 men signed their names. The Seven were hugely outnumbered.

On November 18, the women arrived at Surgeons' Hall on Nicolson Street to take their exams. Also present? A mob of protesters so big it blocked traffic for over an hour. As Sophia recalled, some two hundred men were there "smoking and passing about bottles of whiskey, while they abused us in the foulest possible language." One of the women's student allies managed to open the gate, and the seven gals made a beeline for the anatomy classroom, where they proceeded to take the exam covered in rotten vegetables and mud that had been hurled at them, and "in spite of the yells and howls resounding outside, and the forcible intrusion of a luckless sheep" that had been pushed in by the crowd. "Let it remain," said a certain Dr. Handyside of the poor animal, "it has more sense than those who sent it here." A group of students that the Seven dubbed "the Irish Brigade" escorted the women safely back to their homes and helped them get to and from class without incident for the rest of the week.

But that was far from the end of it. The Surgeons' Hall riot set off an even more vicious cascade of events. First, male students started writing letters to the newspapers in an attempt to justify their actions. (Sophia refused to copy their letters in her memoirs, writing that "the worst of them are really too filthy to quote, but any one interested in such gems of literature" could refer to the papers themselves.) Then, Sophia came straight out and asserted that the riot had been led in part by Professor Christison's drunk assistant—who then sued her for libel. In court, Sophia clarified: "the foul language he used could only be excused on the supposition I heard that he was intoxicated." When Christison took issue with Sophia's "foul language" and the lord provost presiding over the proceeding asked her to withdraw the word "intoxicated," Sophia clarified: "I said it was the only excuse for his conduct. If Dr. Christison prefers that I should say he used the language when sober, I will withdraw the other supposition." The whole courtroom burst into laughter.

The riot, the letters to the newspapers, and the libel case ultimately had the opposite effect that the men of the medical institution had hoped for. The exposure galvanized public support for the Seven across the UK by bringing to light just how terribly the women had been treated by their male colleagues. Edith boosted Sophia's spirits with her support ("bless her!" Sophia later wrote), and articles in papers like the *Scotsman* ("a certain class of medical students are doing their utmost to make the name of medical student synonymous with all that is cowardly and degrading") certainly didn't hurt, either. In 1871, the thousand-strong Committee for Securing a Complete Medical Education for Women in Edinburgh (better known as CSCMEWE; not great with acronyms, these guys) banded together to help the Seven get their degrees.

Yet despite this awesome outpouring of support (and the fact that the women had *earned* their degrees), it was not to be. Basically, university officials decided that they never had the power to admit women in the first place, so, oh well! Thanks for playing! They wouldn't be awarding them their MDs after all. The Seven sought appeals and reversals and reversals *of* reversals, but after two years and several dead ends, they tried to take a different tack. In 1873, Sophia and Isabel headed to London with £100 they had raised from fourteen of their friends and together opened the London School of Medicine for Women. Isabel was elected the organizing secretary, and the curriculum was one of the first in the country to emphasize hygiene as a key component in medicine, with Sophia and Edith both teaching classes on the subject. In its early years, six of the Seven aided the school's development by serving as founders, lecturers, inaugural speakers, and members of the executive committee. At the same time, the women worked to petition the government for women's right to attend UK universities. On August 11, 1876, the Enabling Law was finally passed, decreeing that universities were permitted (though not obligated) to admit women.

Struggling and striving were not limited to the Seven's interactions with outsiders; as happens with all buds at times, the group endured some internal conflict as well. In 1872, Isabel and Sophia got into a public argument after Isabel wrote in the *Scotsman* that Sophia had failed an exam due to "her unselfish devotion to the interests of her fellow students." Sophia wrote to the publication maintaining that she hadn't, actually, thank you very much; Isabel felt as though her friend's rebuke had done "irreparable" damage to their public image. Sophia was regarded as controversial by other groundbreaking women doctors like Elizabeth Garrett and Elizabeth Blackwell, who thought she was too brash and confrontational. But Sophia felt that the harassment the Seven had experienced justified her anger, writing that "if such things were possible in the medical profession, women must, at any cost, force their way into it, for the sake of their sisters, who might otherwise be left at the mercy of such human brutes as" the men who opposed their education.

Despite their occasional clashes, the women of the Edinburgh Seven never stopped supporting each other. In 1877, Sophia and Edith headed to Switzerland, and Emily to Paris, to get their MDs; Matilda and Mary followed Emily two years later. Also in 1877, Ireland opened qualifying examinations for medical licenses with the King and Queen's College of Physicians to women who had earned MDs abroad. Sophia remembered that, long ago, one member of the "Irish Brigade" had told her to visit his home country, where "such scenes [as the riot] would be impossible." The gals wasted no time, and Edith was the first to take the exams in Dublin, qualifying as a real, official doctor in Great Britain. "Miss Pechey has done wonders," Isabel wrote of her friend after she passed. Eventually all except Emily and Helen would do the same.

The Edinburgh Seven went on to lead fascinating lives, both personally and professionally. Sophia remained unmarried (like 80 percent of women doctors in 1911). She set up her own prac-

tice in Edinburgh, moved in with the writer (and likely smooch-
er) Margaret Todd, and, with Helen's help, established the Edinburgh School of Medicine for Women in 1886. Helen married
Alexander Russel, the *Scotsman* editor, in 1871 and decided not
to complete her studies; she and Sophia remained friends. Mary
got hitched to a lawyer who died not even two months later. Both
she and Emily, who settled down with a neurologist who helped
the Seven find a location for clinical instruction, worked as physicians at Elizabeth Garrett's New Hospital for Women in London
and ran their own practices.

Isabel dedicated herself to the London School of Medicine
for Women for thirty years as administrator and was succeeded by her daughter, a surgeon. Edith headed to Mumbai to run
the Cama Hospital for Women and Children, where she helped
manage an outbreak of the actual bubonic plague in 1896. Matilda married a physicist (who was also her cousin, oops) and followed him to a teaching position in Tokyo, where she tutored
women in midwifery (she sarcastically thanked the University of
Edinburgh in the *Scotsman* "for having temporarily forgotten to
exclude ladies from the inestimable advantage of good instruction in medical science"). A talented artist, Matilda also wrote
and illustrated a book of Japanese children's stories, and, recog-
nizing how important female friendship had been to her success,
helped establish clubs for women students in Paris and London.

The Seven challenged, loudly and unapologetically, what the
medical establishment thought women were capable of and what
the government dictated women could do. Sophia sometimes
got a bad rap for her disposition—clearly she was not a sunshine-

and-rainbows kinda gal—but dismissing women as "strident," "harsh," "bossy," whatever, is one of the oldest tricks in the "Get Women To Shut Up" book. What was most important was that Sophia's friends had her back. Isabel called Sophia "the main-spring of the seven years' struggle" to whom they were all "deeply indebted as a result." Edith recalled giving a lecture in Yorkshire which she concluded by expressing her deep sense of gratitude and respect for Sophia, "who had got all the abuse because she had done all the work,—in fact all along she had done the work of three women or ([I said] with a grin at the phalanx of men behind [me]) of ten men!" And the audience loved it. As Edith recalled, it "brought down the house."

Today, it's difficult to imagine that the prospect of a woman practicing medicine would be so unthinkably improper as to cause rioting in the street. Which is probably the very future the Seven dreamed of—one where women doctors are, well, *doctors*, allowed to treat their patients without protest or persecution. At the Royal College of Surgeons on Nicolson Street, the same spot as the Surgeons' Hall riot 150 years ago, you'll find a plaque that simply reads: "The Edinburgh Seven, Britain's First Female Medical Students, 1869–1873." I think Sophia and company would be darn proud—not just to be recognized, but to be honored together, as the unstoppable girl gang that they were. ✦

The Women Scientists of Antarctica

THE RESEARCH TEAM THAT
EXPLORED THE ENDS OF THE EARTH

ACTIVE 20TH CENTURY

On February 1, 1982, sci-fi and fantasy author Ursula K. Le Guin published a short story in the *New Yorker* called "Sur." It is a fictional account of a party of South American women who reach the South Pole in 1909, two years before the first "official" claim of discovery by Roald Amundsen of Norway. The women stay long enough to have a cup of tea and then leave, meticulously covering their tracks so as not to embarrass the men who would get there after them. "Sur" is a particularly remarkable tale not only because Antarctica is famously cruel, cold, and unwelcoming to humanity, but also because, for centuries, it was viewed as the last place on earth where a man could be a man—No Girls Allowed. And although Ursula's story might not be true (though wouldn't it be great if it was?), history is marked by a few small groups of women—always groups—who wouldn't take no for an answer, pulled on their parkas, and took to the great southern cold.

Polar exploration is infamously dangerous today—to say nothing of how things were a century ago. Ice floes trapped ships, temperatures fell far below zero, food shortages were frequent, and death from exposure and starvation was common. Though several early attempts were made to sail to the massive southern-most continent, the so-called Heroic Age of Antarctic Explora-tion really took off at the end of the 1800s and lasted until about the end of the first world war. Militaries and geographical soci-eties all across the Western world were sending men south—and when I say men, I mean only men.

But, occasionally, women managed to find their way there, too. In 1773, a disguised French woman named Louise Séguin was onboard the ship *Roland* when it first entered the Antarctic region. Several unnamed captains' wives accompanied their hus-bands on Antarctic journeys in the late 1800s. In 1839, survivors of a shipwreck, including one female castaway, were rescued from Campbell Island (about 435 miles south of New Zealand's South Island) and passed what was probably mainland Antarctica—but, of course, the captain of the rescuing ships didn't bother to write her name down. In January 1914, when British explorer Er-nest Shackleton was planning his famous *Endurance* expedition, he received a letter from three friends, Peggy Pegrine, Valerie Davey, and Betty Webster, self-described "sporty girls" who were "also gay and bright" [*Author's note:* nice]. They were eager to "don masculine attire" and join Ernest on his trip because, frankly, they did "not see why men should have all the glory." Spoiler: Ernest said no. (And then the mission was a total failure and he died on the next one. Welp!)

The first women to set foot on mainland Antarctica arrived in the 1930s. Ingrid Christensen, whose husband, Lars, was the mega-rich owner of one of the world's largest whaling fleets (and the underwriter of many Norwegian expeditions), brought along her friends Mathilde Wegger and Lillemor Rachlew and her daughter Sofie on a series of trips with lots of seal hunting and photo taking and "great blocks of ice as big as church towers lay[ing] higgledy-piggeldy, five miles deep, jammed tightly together" (according to Lillemor).

Following Ernest's final mission, the Heroic Age faded into a new era (which I like to call the Let's Do Some Serious Science age), the US government sought to study the literal ends of the earth. In February 1956, research facility McMurdo Station opened its doors (and probably shut them really fast, because wind) on the shore of the McMurdo Sound, named for a lieutenant on the intimidatingly named HMS *Terror*. And with that, the government invited a whole bunch of lady scientists to get down there to conduct tests and gather data.

Haha, just kidding! Women visited McMurdo soon after its opening, but not to join in the research. In 1957, US Navy rear admiral George Dufek, who had spent years in the frozen south, convinced the Pan American airline to send a commercial flight to McMurdo as a way to drum up public interest in Antarctica. He was bombarded by requests from women writers, journalists, and pilots to join the flight and found the situation "embarrassing" because McMurdo wouldn't be "quite ready" for women until the station was staffed by equal numbers of women and men. (According to some reports, he may have shouted "Women? Women on the ice? There will be no goddamned women on the ice while I'm [in charge]!" but really, same nasty sentiment whether he couched it in politeness or not.) Despite George's insistence that "if there are any hostesses [on the plane], they're going to be men," on October 15, 1957, Pan Am flight attendants Ruth Kelley and Patricia Hepinstall were onboard the first commercial flight to McMurdo. Ignoring George's orders, Ruth and Pat left the plane and became the first women ever to set foot that far south. For this great honor, the women got to judge a beard-growing contest and joined a dog-sled race that ended up getting canceled when the stopwatch froze.

But change was coming. In the 1950s, the Society of Women Engineers started pushing for more media representation of women scientists. In 1958, the chemist Betty Lou Raskin gave a speech entitled "American Women: Unclaimed Treasures of Science" and called for more encouragement of girls to pursue STEM careers. The following year, the American Council on Women in Science offered a graduate scholarship to women who wanted to return to their studies after having children. By the mid-1960s, women had unquestionably joined the ranks of scientists. In the early years of McMurdo Station, plenty of women were polar scientists, Antarctic scientists, and marine biologists, and they weren't thrilled about being stuck in, say, some laboratory in the Midwest, instead of conducting their studies in Antarctica. The US Navy—which controlled McMurdo Station—was still trying to keep women out of the research center using a flimsy excuse about not having women's bathrooms there. But these scientists, who cared way more about their work than where they'd have to pee, were undeterred.

In 1962, the National Science Foundation (aka the money behind the Navy) accepted a proposal from one Dr. M. A. McWhinnie to join the Antarctic research ship *Eltanin* to study krill, not realizing that "M. A." was actually short for Mary Alice. (Surprise, suckers!) In the 1968–69 summer season, Argentina sent four women scientists—Dr. Irene Bernasconi, Dr. Maria Adeal Caria, Dr. Elena Martinez Fontez, and Dr. Carmen Pujals—to Palmer Station, a research outpost just above the Arctic Circle. "We have wanted all our lives to make this trip," said Irene, a starfish biologist, "to finally touch with our own hands the sea life that until now we have only been able to study as preserved specimens." But McMurdo Station, the largest community in Antarctica, had yet to see its first all-gal scientist team.

"Have you ever seen a female scientist with a parka on? She is virtually indistinguishable from a male scientist with a parka on." So said Colin Bull, the director of Ohio State University's Institute of Polar Studies. Colin had led the first university-sponsored expedition to the Antarctic from New Zealand in 1958—an expedition that geology student Dawn Rodley asked to join, only to be rejected by the US Navy. Since that first expedition, Colin was determined to get a team of women to Antarctica—and, eleven years later, he succeeded. In 1969, the Navy finally approved a team of women researchers from OSU to join the base at McMurdo. "It was really utterly stupid, the whole thing," Colin said, "but we managed to bust it."

The team was to be a small group of women from OSU who would conduct geological research in the almost ice-free Dry Valleys west of McMurdo Sound for the 1969–70 season, getting some brief survival training in the Antarctic backcountry before living out of tents and melting ice for drinking water. Heading up the dream team was geochemist Lois Jones, who wrote her doctoral thesis on chemical ratios in Antarctic rock samples and whom Colin said was "built like a Sherman tank" (goals). Lois invited entomologist and master of science Kay Lindsay and Eileen McSaveney, who'd been the only woman undergraduate in geology at the University of Buffalo before she attended OSU for graduate school. "I thought about it for a while—about half a second—and said yes," Eileen told Marlene Cimons of the National Science Foundation in 2010. "It didn't seem out of the ordinary."

Another scientist on the team dropped out, and suddenly Lois found herself in need of a cook and field assistant. Meanwhile, Terry Lee Tickill, a 19-year-old chemistry undergrad, was desperate to escape from a future filled with dreary laboratories. After reading about a graduate student's Antarctic trip in the school paper, she marched into the university's Institute of Polar Studies and announced that she wanted to go to Antarctica—despite never having traveled farther than 250 miles from home. "The room fell dead silent," she remembered. But when Lois's team had a spot to fill, Colin recommended Terry as a perfect candidate, in part because she "was really good at stripping down a motorbike, or a radio, or a Primus [stove]." Terry knew that her farm upbringing made her a good fit. "Why wouldn't we be able to make it?" she remembered wondering. "It just didn't make sense to me that we couldn't do it. I didn't feel so much pressured [to succeed] as amused that they would think we were so unable to do the same sorts of things the men were."

With Jean Pearson, a *Detroit Free Press* science reporter, the women functioned as a team, working, eating, and bunking together. They tried to make their icy camp life as homey as they could; Eileen remembered that an elementary school had sent them some curtains to use on their trip. "They weren't terribly useful," she said in 2010, "but we did string them on the outside our tents, and photographed them." Lois, the oldest, was the "Mother Hen" of the group, taking care of her team and keeping them safe from the rampant sexism and harassment they endured at the station (unsurprising, but still disappointing). Some of the men hadn't seen a woman in more than a year, which made the atmosphere at the base kind of weird, as you might imagine. Colin remembered getting a letter from one male friend that began: "Dear Colin, Traitor!" because he was so irked that the women were there. In 2009 Terry recalled to Peter Rejcek of the *Antarctic Sun* that she'd been followed around by a man whom she later found literally crying in shock. "I think you're a woman," he told her. Terry said she thought she was, too. "The thing that struck me was how unnatural it was," she said of the men living so long in Antarctica without contact with women.

Of course, freaked-out-slash-predatory dudes were hardly the only dangers the women faced in Antarctica, where people routinely died from poor conditions and the freezing cold. "The wind blew all the time, and there was sand in our boots, sand in our clothes and sand in our food," Terry recalled in 2010. "There was sand in everything. We had oatmeal for breakfast every morning—not because we liked it, but because it was the only thing that was edible with sand in it." Once, the gals were even stranded after a helicopter propeller blade blew off right after takeoff, leaving the women to show the pilots how to survive in the wilderness until a rescue team arrived.

Though still not thrilled about the women's presence at McMurdo, the Navy recognized a potential press opportunity to put an egalitarian spin on the situation and make their program at least appear more progressive. So, on November 12, 1969, they flew the six-member team from OSU and Pam Young, a New Zealand biologist studying in Antarctica, to the South Pole, making them the first women ever to land there. Because the Navy didn't want any one woman to be able to say she'd been the first, the women were made to exit the plane in a line with linked arms. Naturally, the press was there, too; the reporters asked the women if they would be wearing lipstick while they worked (really posing the tough questions, apparently).

When the helicopter finally came to the Dry Valleys to return the women to base on their way back to Ohio, Terry grabbed their box full of rock samples and began lugging it to the chopper. "One of the crew members immediately rushed up and said, 'Let me take that,' and grabbed it," Eileen recalled in 2010 to Cimons of the NSF. "He sank to his knees. I don't think his fellow crew members ever let him forget that." Upon the women's return to base, the military complained that their presence was disruptive, and the scientific community complained when they took more than a year to publish their findings. But Colin Bull always insisted that "they made about the same number of mistakes as a party of four neophyte males would have made—[but] no more." Eileen agreed: "We didn't disgrace ourselves by needing to be rescued, so I presume it made things easier for the next women proposing to go south."

She was super, super right. The following year, Irene Peden, an electrical engineering professor at the University of Washington who studied polar atmosphere, and Julia Vickers, her field assistant from New Zealand, would become the first women to work on the continent's interior. (The women, as ever, were committed to going to Antarctica in groups—plus, it was still a rule.) The Navy and the NSF flat-out told the pair that if they failed, "there won't be another woman on the Antarctic continent for a generation." Their equipment, for *some* reason, never showed up. But still, they didn't fail and their data collection mission went off spectacularly.

Just a few years later, in 1974, 51-year-old Mary Alice McWhinnie—remember her, from the *Eltanin*?—was appointed chief science officer at McMurdo, a position that would require her to "winter over" on the base (i.e., to stay on the base from mid-February to mid-November, the coldest months of the year, during which there are no flights in or out). When someone asked if women really belonged in Antarctica, Mary Alice shot back: "Well, if women are in science and science is in the Antarctic, then women belong there." She called Sister Mary Odile Cahoon, one of her former graduate students, and asked the 45-year-old biologist if she would be interested in accompanying her to the Antarctic to become the first two women to winter over at McMurdo—two women among 128 men. Sister Mary agreed, suspecting that the NSF would be most comfortable having two women who were, shall we say, appropriately mature (I mean, she was a literal nun). Mary Alice and Sister Mary shared everything: a lab, an office, a bedroom. If they were invited someplace, it was always together. "It was a good thing we were friends," Sister Mary said. While in the Antarctic, the Marys studied temperature adaptation on invertebrates and fish, attempting to understand how specific life forms survive in an otherwise barren environment. They would get up between five and seven in the morning, work all day, eat supper, and then work again until midnight in summer, when the sun still had not set.

These historic firsts by the trailblazing Marys and the OSU team before them paved the way for more women to break barriers at the South Pole. In January 1989, 39-year-old Shirley Metz and 24-year-old Tori Murden became the first women to reach the pole overland, on skis, completing a journey of more than 700 miles. With the sun never setting, the women skied nine hours a day, falling dozens of times and taking breaks of only five minutes so as not to freeze in -77 degrees Fahrenheit. In 1993, Minnesota teacher Ann Bancroft cashed in on the five years of her life and a bunch of the personal finances that she'd spent on training, and led the first all-women expedition to the South Pole on skis. (A decade later, she and fellow teacher Liv Arneson of Norway became the first women to ski across the continent unaided.) By 1997, nearly 40 percent of the workers at McMurdo were women. Men who've spent twenty seasons at the base think having women around makes for a more positive environment. And in 2016, seventy-six women, the largest all-lady expedition ever, decided to band together and head out from Ushuaia, Argentina, on an Antarctic trip that served as the launch of what they called the Homeward Bound initiative, a program that aims to create a network of 1,000 women to promote women in science and increase awareness of the ravages of climate change. Today, the joke is that to get a date from a woman at McMurdo, you just have to *be* a woman at McMurdo—a place that draws strong-bodied and strong-minded independent women from all across the globe.

With "Sur," Ursula K. Le Guin encouraged readers to imagine that the first people to set foot on the South Pole were women, who came and went quietly, for their gratification only, so as not to upset the delicate male ego. In fact, the first women to trek to the last untouched place on earth did so loudly and strongly, supporting one another as friends and scientists. Lois and her team knew that their work was important not only for scientific research, but also for the historical record. The next group of women to reach Antarctica would, hopefully, struggle less, and the ones after them, less still. And they would owe it, in part, to the teamwork and friendship of all the Antarctic women who came before them. ✦

The West Area Computers

THE BLACK WOMEN MATHEMATICIANS
WHO PUT A MAN ON THE MOON

ACTIVE 20TH CENTURY

Many girls are raised to believe they can be anything, achieve anything, *do* anything that boys can do. But too often, society sends girls another message: that there's a limit on their achievements, whether it's a professional glass ceiling or fields where women supposedly don't belong. And limiting stereotypes affect women of color even more strongly, having to fight racism in addition to misogyny. Nevertheless, the West Area Computers fought for what they wanted—to power a rocket to the moon by working in a field almost entirely dominated by men at a time in American history when discrimination was legal. And they did it. *Together.*

In 1943, recent college grad Kathryn Peddrew had run into a dead end. This 21-year-old Black woman who had been raised to believe she could be whatever she dreamed wanted to become a chemist and a scholar. After graduation, she planned to join her Storer College professor in New Guinea to research hearing loss caused by quinine, a medicine used to treat malaria. But the university told her that there were simply no *facilities* for women in New Guinea (why is where women scientists pee such an issue?), and so the position couldn't be hers. Looking for alternatives, Kathryn noticed an ad for a job in the chemistry division at NACA—the National Advisory Committee for Aeronautics—in Hampton, Virginia. She applied and was hired within the year. She boarded a train in West Virginia that she thought was bound for Hampton, only to be sold a ticket to Newport News, ten miles away from her destination, by a stationmaster who had no idea where Hampton was. Eventually, in summer 1953, she arrived at NACA's Langley Research Laboratory, ready to do some chemistry. But on her first day, Kathryn was shuttled to a different department, called the West Area Computers. There were no Black employees in the chemistry division, she was told.

So what was this mysterious West Area? Well, for starters, NACA was having something of a personnel crisis, like basically every employer in the country: men kept joining, or being drafted into, the armed forces. Where once Langley's rooms were full of men scribbling equations, there were now empty chairs and a whole lot of unsolved math. Leaving the math unsolved wasn't an option; given the literal life-and-death nature of wartime aeronautics projects, the calculations had to be done exactly correctly. So just plug it into a computer, right? Nope: computers as we know them today weren't a thing yet. The Langley Research Laboratory employed a group of so-called human computers, who would do the math and deliver the results to busy engineers. As World War II loomed, this computing work had become essential to keeping American aeronautics at the cutting edge. With no technological solution yet available, and most of the dudes off to battle, NACA had to start recruiting women.

The first all-female computing pool at Langley was formed in 1935, its size steadily increasing as the war approached. Unsurprisingly, the "girls," as they were known, were not exactly welcomed with open arms by their male coworkers. But the male engineers, who were at first appalled by the idea of buying $500 Friden calculating machines (necessary to calculate multiplications and square roots) for tiny-brained silly women, quickly realized that the girls in the pool were just plain better at doing the math than the male engineers. And the women did a *lot* of work; they spent their days reading film, plotting data, and completing calculations in the central pool, wind tunnel, or research divisions. With the help of slide rules and magnifying glasses, they compiled and graphed data collected from wind tunnel tests and plane prototypes. Combine that crucial work with the money NACA was saving by designating the women as "subprofessional" computers instead of "professional" mathematicians, and you can see why the agency started to dig having them around: they were effectively better *and* cheaper.

By the end of World War II, the women's computing department at Langley had grown from fewer than one hundred employees to more than one thousand, accounting for nearly a third of the Langley staff. To house new hires, NACA built Anne

Wythe Hall in 1943, a dormitory that provided daycare, right outside the facility gates.

But by 1943, the year Kathryn Peddrew arrived, Langley's head computer, Virginia Tucker, had pretty much already run out of qualified women to hire on the East Coast. She was even courting young women who were just entering college, in the hopes that they might want to forgo their education for an immediate job in computing. The gig was pretty plum; a woman with a bachelor's degree in math or science who aced the Civil Service Examination could be hired as either a junior computer, earning around $1,440 a year, or a chief computer, with an annual salary of about $3,200 (which, although it was way less than what men made, was still about triple a teacher's salary at the time). Advertisements for the jobs with cheerfully borderline-sexist copy proclaimed: "Reduce your household duties! Women who are not afraid to roll up their sleeves and do jobs previously filled by men should call the Langley Memorial Aeronautical Laboratory." Yet Virginia still had spots to fill. Why? Well, one of the unspoken "qualifications" for the job was that the women be white.

Luckily for Virginia, the socialist and civil rights leader A. Philip Randolph had fought hard against workplace discrimination, and his efforts were rewarded when President Roosevelt signed Executive Orders 8802 and 9346, in 1941 and 1943 respectively, abolishing segregation in the defense industry and establishing the Fair Employment Practices Committee to help defend against racial discrimination in the workplace. By the mid-'40s, Langley saw computing applications rolling in from often over-qualified women applicants who had graduated from historically Black colleges and universities like Howard, West Virginia State, and the local Hampton Institute.

In 1940, only 2 percent of Black women had degrees, and over half of them would go on to be employed as teachers. These prospective computers were the first Black women in America to seek employment as mathematicians. Hiring them offered Virginia a solution to her staffing problem—but the start of another one. Executive orders notwithstanding, this was still midcentury Virginia—public racial segregation (Jim Crow) laws were enforced throughout the South until the mid-'60s. So in 1940, on the other side of State Highway 134, a mile away from the wind tunnels, labs, and offices of white female staff, NACA began constructing a new facility, known as the West Area. As it expanded, NACA purchased land from the Wythe family, who had owned the adjacent plot since 1771 and built Chesterville Plantation on it. (As of 1950, the land was still registered to the state as a plantation—1950!). It was in the old plantation boundaries of the West Area that the Black computers—the West Area Computers—of NACA would work, and where Kathryn Peddrew started a job she'd never anticipated.

In the West Area, Kathryn met 36-year-old Miriam Daniel Mann, also a chemistry major. Her husband was a professor at Hampton Institute, and Miriam often brought her math problems home, where she'd talk them out with her daughter at the dining room table. Joining them was Dorothy Vaughan, three years younger than Miriam, who came to NACA after working as a high-school math teacher and struggling to find suitable housing for her family. In 1949, after the West Area Computers had spent years under the management of Margery Hannah and Blanche Sponsler (both white women), Dorothy broke boundaries by becoming the group's first Black head, as well as the very first Black supervisor in all of NACA, leading a team that included Kathryn and Miriam. While in that position, Dorothy campaigned tirelessly for promotions and raises for her employees. "I changed what I could," Dorothy told *Hidden Figures* author Margot Lee Shetterly, "and what I couldn't, I endured."

The next computer to join the team was Mary Jackson, a hometown girl from Hampton who arrived at Langley in 1951, at age 30, with a dual degree in math and physical science from Hampton Institute. After working as a math teacher, receptionist, bookkeeper, stay-at-home mom, and army secretary, Mary found her way into Dorothy's computing pool as a wind-tunnel and flight-test specialist. Annie Easley joined in the mid-1950s and said of the discrimination she faced, "my thing is, if I can't work with you, I will work around you. I was not about to be discouraged that I'd walk away." She eventually became the first woman at Langley to wear pants to work.

Thirty-five-year-old Katherine Johnson rounded out the team in 1953. Born on August 26, 1918 (that's Women's Equality Day, for those of you keeping track), Katherine was a math prodigy who started high school early on the West Virginia State College campus (her hometown didn't offer schooling for Black kids past the eighth grade) and graduated with honors from that same college by age 18, mentored by W. W. Schieffelin Claytor, the third Black math PhD recipient in the country. After a brief stint as a teacher, Katherine returned to West Virginia State;

she'd been selected by the school's president as the first Black woman to attend its newly integrated grad program. One of her professors said she would make a good research mathematician, she remembered. "I said, 'Where will I get a job?' And he said, 'That will be your problem.' And I said, 'What do they do?' And he said, 'You'll find out.'"

Instead of graduating, Katherine did pretty much what you did at that time—worked as a teacher, then became a stay-at-home mom to her three daughters, you know the drill. While on vacation in Newport News, she "heard that Langley was looking for black women computers," Katherine recalled, and soon she found herself in Dorothy's West Area section, finally putting her incredible math skills to the test. Feeling like she was in "seventh heaven," Katherine moved from a temporary position to full-time in just two weeks. Dorothy assigned her to the Flight Research Division, and she worked hard on flight test data analysis until her husband died from cancer in 1956. "The NACA days were just delightful," Katherine would remember of the professional atmosphere in which she worked.

The West Area Computers knew one another by their first names, worked together well on a twenty-four-hour shift schedule, and were friends outside the office. And in addition to the satisfaction of getting to work with buds, Langley paid white and Black women computers similar wages. Mary Jackson earned $3,410 a year (equivalent today to about $32,000) when she started in 1951. But equivalent pay was about where equality began and ended for the West Area Computers; not only did they still make less than half of what newly hired male engineers took home, they also were almost entirely segregated from their white counterparts, many of whom weren't even aware of their existence. Before starting work, the West Area Computers were required to take a chemistry course at Hampton Institute, although their credentials were often more impressive than those of white women who applied. The West Area Computers worked in separate offices and used separate bathrooms and ate either in a "colored" dining room, whose entrance was on the opposite side of the building from the white dining room, or at a single table in the back of the white dining room marked with a white-cardboard sign that read COLORED (which Miriam snatched off the table every time it appeared until finally it stopped being replaced). Their assigned projects were often just tedious overflow from the white computers, and they were prohibited from living in Anne Wythe Hall, leaving them to find housing on their own in Hampton, which proved a great challenge for some of the women who had relocated to the area for their jobs.

But the brilliant West Area Computers didn't let discrimination stop them from looking for opportunities. After two years with the computers, Mary started to work in the Supersonic Pressure Tunnel for Kazimierz Czarnecki, an engineer who evidently enjoyed being stuck in a four-by-four-foot square high-powered wind tunnel all day. Kazimierz was a big fan of Mary and wanted her to become an engineer. However, to do so, she'd have to take graduate-level evening courses in math and physics offered by the University of Virginia at Hampton High School. A white high school. You may be seeing the problem here: Mary was Black. The high school was white. She still wanted to become an engineer.

With her friends encouraging her to follow her dreams and help break down the barriers that plagued them all, Mary was able to harness her Heimdall-sized inner strength. She marched before the City of Hampton and asked for special permission to attend the classes at Hampton High, which she was granted. Trying her best not to care about the stares she got from her fellow students—mostly men, entirely white—Mary completed her coursework. In 1958, at age 37, she became the first Black female Engineer at NACA and coauthored her first paper with her mentor, Kazimierz. In the remainder of her time as a NACA engineer, Mary paid it forward to other West Area Computer gals, working as a kind of career counselor and advising them on courses and assignments to take on to put them in the best position for promotion to engineer.

Now, while the West Area Computers were working hard, moving up, seizing opportunities, doing math, and generally crushing it as a team, the Soviets had successfully launched Sputnik, the first real honest-to-goodness satellite from Earth, in October 1957. The Space Race between the USSR and the US was on, and NACA was on the front lines. In 1958, Katherine contributed to the math for a space-technology lecture series in the Flight Research Division and the Pilotless Aircraft Research Division about how to safely get a payload into orbit and back to Earth again (we're not sure exactly what parts of the math are hers, because NACA didn't credit her contributions, of course). Many engineers from these two divisions went on to form NACA's Space Task Group (a name so cool it should probably belong to a hip all-girl band). The group's job was to figure out how to get fragile, tiny humans into space without incinerating their fragile, tiny bodies, and, as a top computer, Katherine "came along with the program." That same year, under President Eisenhower's National Aeronautics and Space Act, NACA officially became the National Aeronautics and Space Administration, better known as NASA.

That same year, segregated facilities were mostly abolished at Langley (racial segregation had been declared unconstitutional in 1954). Dorothy and the rest of the West Area Computers joined the Analysis and Computation Division, where Black and white men and women worked together using the first *electronic* computers. Miriam's daughter recalled in 2011 that her mother "was excited when the first real computer was installed and it was larger than today's walk-in closets." Mary, meanwhile, remembered that even after integration, the former West Area Computers still were expected to "know which restrooms were for which race." Though desegregation was ultimately an improvement, this was a trying time of transition at NASA. But, with the help of their strong bonds of supportive friendship, the West Area Computers continued to rock at rockets.

Another historic first came two years later, in 1960: Katherine became the first woman from the Flight Research Division to be credited by name as co-author on a report about the landing location of orbital spacecrafts. "We wrote our own textbook," she said of the project, "because there was no other text about space." But with the barrier-breaking came isolation; as Katherine put it, she "went where women had never been" and was frequently "the only woman in such meetings." Nevertheless, she found herself able to do "a lot of the early work on space for that reason." She worked on the 1961 Freedom 7 mission, the first time America sent a human into space, ensuring that astronaut Alan Shepard landed exactly where he was supposed to on his return voyage. "Early on," Katherine remembered, "when they said they wanted the capsule to come down at a certain place, they were trying to compute when it should start. I said, 'Let me do it. You tell me when you want it and where you want it to land, and I'll do it backwards and tell you when to take off.' That was my forte."

Two years later, NASA was preparing for John Glenn to orbit Earth. Electronic computers across the globe in Washington DC, Cape Canaveral, and Bermuda had been programmed with the math that would predict the exact location of the Friendship 7 capsule at each moment of the trip. But John was no fool; he knew that those machines were no replacement for humans. Before takeoff, he demanded that NASA "get the girl" to check all the calculations. Katherine later remembered what John said to the team of her work as he prepared for his spaceflight: "If she says they're good, then I'm ready to go." Best of all, it was a team effort: Miriam worked on the math that would help dock John's ship in space.

John's successful orbit and safe return put America firmly ahead in the Space Race—and validated Katherine's and Miriam's hard work. (Miriam was even at the Langley labs when John came to show his appreciation for her team's work on his Mercury 7 spaceflight.) But that spaceflight was hardly the end of the program. In 1969, Katherine, along with the rest of the West Area Computers, watched Neil Armstrong set foot on the moon—another milestone she had helped achieve. "I had done the calculations and knew they were correct," she recalled. "But just like driving [to Hampton] from Williamsburg this morning, anything could happen." In other words, anything could have gone wrong—but nothing did. Neil took that first step backed by a team of brilliant Black women who had helped make it happen.

The moon landing was just the beginning of the computers' legacy. Kathryn worked at NASA for thirty-three years, mostly in the Instrument Research Division. Annie stayed on for thirty-four years and wrote the code for the Centaur, a rocket component that helps launch vessels into space, which has been used in over 200 takeoffs. Miriam retired for health reasons in 1966 but was always proud of her work on John Glenn's mission. Dorothy became an expert in the Fortran computing language and worked until her retirement in 1971; her son now works for NASA's computer division. Mary worked as an engineer for nearly twenty years, studying the way air moves around planes; yet despite three decades of hard work, she was never able to move into a management role. Instead of letting her frustration get the best of her, Mary shifted gears and, at age 58, took a demotion to become an Equal Opportunity Specialist heading up Langley's Federal Women's and Affirmative Action Programs in Washington DC, continuing the legacy of her original group of West Area Computers. She worked in that capacity for six years, until her retirement, getting as many women at NASA hired and promoted in math, engineering, and science as she possibly could.

Katherine, the woman whose sharp math skills helped get a man on the moon, continued at Langley until her retirement in

1986, working on the Space Shuttle and Earth Resources Satellite programs as well as on over two dozen research reports. "I found what I was looking for at Langley," she said in 2008. "I went to work every day for thirty-three years happy." Katherine has received honorary doctorates, awards, and honors, and in 2015, at the age of 97, she received the highest honor a US civilian can hope for: the Presidential Medal of Freedom, awarded by President Barack Obama.

As a powerful, smart, and amazingly hardworking bunch of women, the West Area Computers opened the door for Black women across America to be taken seriously as mathematicians, colleagues, and coworkers. Though Katherine never wanted to make a big deal out of it (as she told Margot Lee Shetterly again and again: "I was just doing my job"), their teamwork was unprecedented and remarkable, not only because of the achievements made possible by their calculations, but also because as a group they were able to work together and lift one another up. The West Area Computers became like sisters during their time at Langley; their children are still friends today. Miriam and Dorothy attended concerts together. They bonded with Kathryn over life as working moms, holding annual extended family picnics; they ate lunch together, weathered hardships together, fangirled over Uhura together. They won the Space Race and landed a man on the moon. But most of all, they gave the next generation of marginalized women in STEM a precedent for their dreams, proving that nothing is impossible with the support of your community and your friends. As Annie told an oral historian in 2001, "We were a team. We were always a team." ✦

CHAPTER 5

ARTIST SQUADS

Throughout history, all across the world, women have formed literary and musical gangs whose work—both because of what it said and because it was women doing the sayin'—changed the world. They prove that although fighting for change is possible, you don't have to take up arms for progress. Conquering minds can be just as important as chopping someone's head off (although head-chopping is still pretty rad, don't get me wrong). Let's learn about some of the most interesting artistic girl groups the globe has ever known.

The Trobairitz

*THE FEMINIST MUSICIANS
WHO ROCKED MEDIEVAL FRANCE*

ACTIVE CIRCA 1180-1230

When you think of badass, barrier-busting women's bands, you probably picture some landmark groups of the modern era like Bikini Kill, Salt-N-Pepa, or Sleater-Kinney. But that punk-rock girl power ethos—standing up to society, taking on a male-dominated art form, and expressing a no-holds-barred cry for freedom—has existed pretty much as long as women have had instruments. Even when those instruments were, like, lutes and harps. Yep, in medieval Europe, the resident lady rockers were shredding on the courtly stage and taking patriarchal conventions to task in their lyrics. Put your hands in the air for . . . the trobairitz of Occitania!

These ladies of the Occitan courts—the first women composers of secular music in Europe—weren't satisfied being the objects of someone else's songs. They started to write their own poems in response to the restrictively sexist popular jams of the time. Unlike troubadours, male lyrical poets and poet-musicians who made a livelihood from their music, the trobairitz weren't out to make money. They were writing for themselves and no one else. Though there was no gendered distinction made between male and female poets at the time, today we call these gals the trobairitz (basically "women who compose," in Old Occitan).

To understand why these women were so revolutionary, it helps to have a little background in the arts scene of the time. Occitania, the historical region that made up a big chunk of what is now southern France and smaller bits of modern-day Catalonia, Monaco, and Italy, was lucky enough to have a fifty-year period, a so-called Golden Interlude, from roughly 1180 to 1230, during which women's rights got a serious boost, more than other European women would see for centuries to come.

See, France as we know it today didn't spring forth from the earth fully bordered and ready to cheese; until well into the first millennium, northern France and southern France were vastly different in language, religion, and culture. The south of France (including Aquitaine and Gascony in the southwest, Languedoc in the central south, and Provence in the southeast) fell under the Occitanian banner. After the ninth century, Occitania existed as a loose collection of independent duchies, kingdoms, and counties, united less by borders than by shared customs and language. But things were still a bit of a mess, to put it lightly. In addition to infighting between feudal duchies and kingdoms trying to wrest power from one another, there was England busting in to cause trouble (as usual), with kings from Henry I at the end of the eleventh century to Edward III in the fourteenth century going to war over land claims from Normandy in the far north of France all the way down to Aquitaine in the Occitanian south. And we can't forget about the good ol' Crusades, the first of which, in 1096, saw the pope sending men from across Europe into the Middle East for "saving" (or "murdering," but, you know, semantics to the medieval pope, I guess); this was followed by the Second Crusade in 1147, and so on all the way to the Eighth Crusade in 1270. That's, obviously, going to mean a high death toll for the men being sent from France.

But the women were more than equipped to pick up the slack. As the Golden Interlude began, Occitania went back to many of the Roman-influenced laws they had followed prior to the tenth century, which allowed women not only to inherit property but also to dispose of wealth and land. Your husband got shipped off to war? No problem; your feudal fiefdom was yours to manage or sell as you pleased. So, theoretically, women had the right to refuse a marriage offer, because they didn't need men to survive. And since the Golden Interlude began before the establishment of universities (which would end up being for men only, to keep women uneducated and oppressed), women with money had access to tutors and the best teachers in convents. Family names were handed down through the matrilineal line in eleventh-century Occitan twice as often as they were in the north, a tradition that might have stemmed from the area's former Barbarian kingdom, where sexual promiscuity had been a-okay, and it was much easier to keep track of who your mom was than your dad. There were whole generations of highly educated women running households, owning land, and controlling fief-doms. This very specific confluence of no men + educated women + Roman and Barbarian history saw women in the 1180–1230 period doing pretty okay for themselves.

But it wasn't just "all the men getting killed" and some egal-itarian law systems that gave women their relative dominance. Believe it or not, religion also gave them a leg up. See, a *lot* of the people of Occitania, particularly in the Languedoc region, weren't Catholics but Cathars, Christians with a determinedly un-Catholic bent who believed that God was lawful good and everything of the physical world was chaotic evil. Individual re-sponsibility was big for the Cathars; *prix* and *parage* (that's pride and courtesy to you and me) were foundational concepts, and te-nets like vegetarianism, religious and racial tolerance, class con-sciousness, and—most excellently—equality between men and women were also part of their faith. The Cathars weren't partic-ularly keen on the constraints of marriage; they thought wom-en should be uplifted both socially and morally. They were more about peace than war and were generally more tolerant than your average European at the time. Plus, women could actively participate in the Cathar ministry, becoming prefects who could preach, practice medicine, and deliver the sacrament; nearly half of all named Cathar preachers were women. They were kind of progressive forest preachers who were a little ahead of the curve on the social justice front, and Occitania was all about it. So, as with all cultural moments like the Golden Interlude, a conflu-ence of factors explained the surge in women's independence, but Cathar beliefs were a biggie.

With all those love-ins and tasty meatless snacks, it might be hard to see exactly what these trobairitz girls had to rebel against. But make no mistake: there was still some constrainin' going on in the form of *fin'amors*, the predominant artistic ethos of the age that was pretty keen on women just standing still and looking pretty. *Fin'amors*, or "courtly love," is both super-essential to the poems and songs of this era and also super-difficult to describe in modern terms. (Imagine trying to get someone from 1,000 years in the future to understand what "Netflix and chill" means.) But in very broad strokes, *fin'amors* is a conception of love that involves Very Noble Dudes doing good deeds to win the affections of Very Beautiful Ladies. Intertwined with the moral loftiness was a thread of illicit behavior and sneaking around (think of star-crossed Tristan and Isolde, or Lancelot and Guinevere gettin' it on behind King Arthur's back) and a hefty dose of lovesickness and suffering. Basically, *fin'amors* is part artistic convention, part gender theory, and part philosophy, all of which permeated the works of the popular (male) poets of the time, known as troubadours. Though the initial attraction between troubadour and the lady he wrote about—the specific object of his affection was usually couched in anonymity—might have been sexual, *fin'amors* was also about romantic, emotional love, something that just didn't exist between men and women in marriages designed to heighten power or political strategy. Rules of *fin'amors* varied, ranging from arguably progressive (it's chill to love two people at once; you can love someone you're not married to) to horrific (it's totally cool to rape peasant girls because they like it, actually).

Troubadour poetry was, in a word, extra. The first secular Western poetry on record, posed mostly in questions, it's all about nobility and chivalry and suffering and "I'll just die if she doesn't love me back." Troubadours performed their original songs in front of the Occitan courts loudly and vivaciously. They were bops for the times. For the troubadours, love was both transcendental and destructive; it made you a better person while also making you feel like trash, an idea about romantic love to which we still cling (listen to, like, any pop song, seriously).

The women of troubadour songs were typically anonymous and presented as archetypes rather than individuals: unnamed *domnas* (the perfect wife, lady, and mistress of the household who is having sex with someone other than the troubadour), *femnas* (the sexy but virginal daughter who can't have sex with anyone), or *midons* (literally "lord," a third gender; an idealized combination of *domna* and *femna* that was meant to flatter the woman and represent the "perfect" simultaneously sexual and virginal gal for the troubadour).

But though the poems are ostensibly about the troubadour's love for a woman, there's an agenda at work here, and not the kind that the liberated women of Occitania were into. At around age 12 to 15, noble Occitanian girls were usually married to men of the same class who were at home either a lot, a little, or not at all depending on wars and such. However, given that Occitanian culture valued individual political power, men of the lower and merchant classes also wanted a shot at some upper-crust courtly intrigue (and money). For the men of Occitania, *fin'amors* created a kind of real-world social game in which the goal was to win the affection of either a feudal lord's wife or his virgin daughter. That, and as a great way to brag about just how great the man himself was.

In showing off his superhuman ability to suffer for love, the troubadour was basically trying to prove himself honorable and committed enough for his "perfect" woman. But it's the "perfect" that's the problem here. Isn't the troubadour just *amazing* for being so nice and worthy of love from such perfection? And the woman *must* control all the power in the relationship, no matter who or what kind of person she is IRL, since it's up to her whether she accepts the troubadour's favor (which is basically some Ye Olde Men's Rights ish). For actual living, breathing, women, *fin'amors* poems had little to say that was relatable. So, as the Golden Interlude kicked off in the late 1100s, the women of Occitania started to speak up and rock out.

The poetry of the trobairitz, like that of the troubadours, dealt in the tropes of *fin'amors*, but instead of praising it, the women wrote about how the system that claimed to idolize them in fact was garbage that held them down. And like the troubadours, the trobairitz didn't just write these poems and send them to their dudes in secret; they got up in front of the Occitan courts and sang them just as the troubadours did, often outright naming the men in their songs instead of keeping them anonymous, continuing the discussion of *fin'amors* while actively critiquing it. The translator and scholar Claudia Keelan compares the trobairitz and their songs to hip-hop, but I'd say they're also like Middle Ages Riot Grrrls or the Runaways or Blondie. It was pretty dang punk-rock to fight back against an establishment that expected you to sit down and be quiet; against an encroaching Catholic church that didn't want you making secular music or doing anything at all but passionlessly making babies; against men who thought of you as an object instead of as a person. (The more the songs change, the more they stay the same, huh?)

Today, scholars count between fifteen and fifty trobairitz (compared to over 450 troubadours), either through their surviving songs or through references to women writers with lost works in the poems, biographies, or critiques of other troubadours and trobairitz. In fancy books made for rich Italian patrons called *chansonniers* (songbooks), women's work makes up about 2 percent of poems. I say "about 2 percent" because it's art and everything is subjective: the speaker in the poem is usually the person who wrote the poem, but it's sometimes hard to tell if a speaker is fictitious (some man writing from an invented woman's perspective), or if the anonymous poems traditionally attributed to men were actually written by women (and many likely were). Some biographical information on the trobairitz survives through *vidas* (biographies of poets, which use the same language to describe both troubadours and trobairitz: beautiful, charming, noble, educated) and *razos* (explanations and commentaries on another's poem), though these were often written later and tend to be embellished or fabricated.

Of the many forms of troubadour poetry, the trobairitz wrote mostly *cansos* (love poems) and *tensos* (debate poems, written by two different people expressing different points of view). Using the same techniques as the troubadours in order to best undermine them (satire!), trobairitz *tensos* show the reader a glimpse of a group of girls who wanted to love, but felt trapped by the system, by expectations, by the fear of unwanted pregnancy or getting a bad reputation. These girls do not put Occitanian men on a pedestal; they're more concerned about finding men who show faithfulness, trustworthiness, and emotion and don't just, you know, sing about it. The Comtessa de Dia, Clara d'Anduza, Lombarda, Tibors, Azalais de Procairages, Domna H., Castelloza, Garsenda Countess of Provence, and Gaudairenca—these are all gals we know were trobairitz in the Golden Interlude, some of whom have surviving poems. (One by an anonymous woman that I'm particularly fond of is simply titled "I Am So Pretty and I Don't Love My Husband Any More.")

But there's one tenso that's a particularly excellent jam. It was written by three women: Alais, Iselda, and Carenza. Probably composed near the end of the Golden Interlude, closer to the mid-1200s, "Na Carenza al bel cors avinenz" (named after its first line) survives in only one book, a *chansonnier* in poor condition. The poem is written by two young sisters, Alais and Iselda, and addressed to an older, more experienced lady, Carenza. Basically, Alais is like, "Lady Carenza, you're so pretty and experienced, can you give us two sisters some advice? Should I stay unmarried? That would be awesome, since making babies is unappealing—but also, being husbandless seems like a lot of trouble." And Carenza is like, "Both of you gals are educated, beautiful, young, and your skin is so clear. If you want good offspring, you should take a husband who is crowned with knowledge, and he'll give you that glorious progeny. Honestly though, women are held back by whomever they marry." Then Iselda is like, "Well, I think I *would* dig a husband, actually; but having a baby is like punishment, because my boobs and stomach are going to get all saggy and I'm not down with that." To which Carenza responds, "Oh, you two, just remember me when you're in the protecting shadow and beg the glorious one that at parting I may remain near you."

Just . . . *yes* to everything that's happening here. What's so revolutionary and punk rock about this *tenso* is that, even though the women are talking about marriage, it's not marriage in terms of *fin'amors*. Their own future, not the nobility of some dude, is what's at stake. The final stanza even passes the Bechdel test!

Interestingly, the Occitanians didn't really have words to describe what we think of as "friendship." As far as the lexicon goes, that kind of nonfamilial relationship between women didn't exist in the *fin'amors* courts of medieval France. However, this poem shows that even without a neatly labeled concept like we have today, Middle Ages friendship was the real deal: two teenage sisters seeking the advice of an older, wiser woman on how they should live out their days. (Two teenaged sisters who are beautiful, intelligent, and more focused on their own happiness than that of any man to boot.)

Scholars, being scholars, argue about nearly every aspect of this poem, including who wrote it. Is it two sisters named Alais and Iselda, as the opening lines suggest? Is it just Alais, who speaks through the whole poem for both her and her sister? Or is Alais and Iselda (from "Na Alais i na Iselda" in the original Old Occitan, "Na" being an honorific like "Ms." and "i" meaning "and") a mistranslation of "Na Alaisina Iselda," just one girl? Are the women not real people but actually stand-ins for tropes—Carenza the virgin, Alais the peasant, and Iselda the noble? Then there's the mystery of Carenza's answer: is she telling the girls to join a convent and marry God? The poem was written around the mid-thirteenth century, when the Catholic church had already started to stamp out the Cathars and gain control of Occitainia, so the church's presence might have colored the bent of the narrative. Or is the poem influenced by the Cathars, who hated marriage and wanted people to abandon materialism? Or is Carenza telling the girls to marry a learned man, who will appreciate her virginity and give her a good son? Or is the *tenso* a satire of women who wanted to enter a convent to preserve their beauty?

Ultimately, as with all old-timey writing (and art in general), no one answer is correct. We can never know who wrote the *tenso* or what the intention was behind its writing. But in art, intent matters less than the way in which people interpret it, and we can interpret this poem as being about two young women trying to find their way in the world and using art to get out all their feelings. The Catholic church didn't want women to exist without childbearing, and Alais and Iselda would rather talk about love and sex and artistic and educational fulfillment outside of the bonds of traditional marriage. They recognize that taking a husband and having kids means a lot of sacrifice (of your body, your emotions, your mind, and your time), and they're looking for another way to go. Carenza, the older woman, challenges the younger women to think about her strange and often contradictory advice and to chart their own path. Alais and Iselda seem to me like two pretty darn progressive women who want to be able to smooch a dude without getting pregnant or giving up their individual lives. And Carenza sounds like the woman who wishes she'd had that option available to her too. For 1220s France, it's pretty inspirational.

Alas, this awesome age of punk rock and women's rights and tolerance wouldn't last forever. In 1209, Pope Innocent III (nice ironic name, dude) and the northern French court sent the Inquisition to Occitania and spent the next twenty years attempting to crush the Cathars, along with any Occitan counts and dukes who showed them sympathy. By 1229, the Albigensian Crusade, as the Catholics called it (after the city of Albi where many Cathars lived), was over, despite many Cathar women having helped fortify Toulouse and Beaucaire, up to and including firing catapults from behind the walls. The northern French crown took control of Occitania and wasted no time crushing the culture that had sprung up around the Mediterranean, taking over provinces and forcing non-Catholic stragglers to swear loyalty or die. As a result of this takeover and the arrival of the Black Death in 1348, Occitanian and troubadour culture had crumbled by the mid-fourteenth century. Old Occitanian poetry survives to this day, as do—for better or worse—the ideals of courtly love that the troubadours invented so many centuries ago. But so, too, does the drive of women to push back against expectation with their own art. So rather than hold on to chivalry, or nobility, or judging women against some unattainable, dehumanizing ideal, let's do like the trobairitz, who defied expectations and expressed how they felt through some truly bangin' tunes. Rock on, ladies. ✦

The Blue Stockings Society

THE LITERARY LADIES OF LONDON

ACTIVE CIRCA 1750–1790

More than a century before the Edinburgh Seven would fight for women's admittance to medical school and gender equality in education (see page 166), one small group of women in the United Kingdom would lay the foundation for that very fight. The eighteenth-century Blue Stockings were rich, fancy, pretty, and bored as hell. Fortunately, sometimes people born into privilege actually use their money for the sake of the greater good, and such was the case with our lovely Blue Stockings, the first English literary society both by and for women.

The early 1750s were a great time if you were a wealthy white aristocratic dude in Europe, especially in Britain. Incomes were up, prices were down, colonies were loyal to the crown and dutifully sending sugar and cotton and spices back to the empire, colonies were still behaving according to plan (the plan being "sending tons of sugar and cotton and spices back to the empire, thx"), colonialists were enjoying profits on those exports, and no one would be talking about revolution for another few years. This was an extremely all-play-and-no-work decade, and the lifestyles of the rich and fabulously powdered betrayed it. Ever seen those brocade gowns with hoop skirts that extend so far out to the sides that women had to turn sideways to fit through doors? That's the 1750s. (Sitting down? Never heard of her.)

All this excess wealth tended to lead to an excess of time for Britain's upper classes. If your money is guaranteed to flow in constantly from your thousands of colonial wage-slaves, what's a person to do all day? Help the poor? Heck nah! Gamble it all away recklessly instead, of course! Card games, horse races, cockfights—all these (and more!) games of chance were popular with the midcentury elites. When they weren't throwing away their fortunes, the upper classes headed to the theater or to extravagant dances. If you and I were betting men, like the ones in 1750s Britain, we might be tempted to call this a decade of distractions meant to keep the wealthy from considering the consequences of things like owning nations, watching their countrymen get hungrier and hungrier, and overhearing the early rumblings of revolution but desperately trying to ignore them. It's just a thought.

These distractions weren't limited to one gender—in fact, in a fit of seeming egalitarianism, women were regulars at the card tables just as often as their husbands. In an 1881 *Belgravia* magazine article entitled "The Queen of the Blue-Stockings," writer

H. Barton Baker observed that in this period, "people seemed to have no other object in life than to meet every evening to shuffle cards to win or lose money" and that "young women—mere girls—were as deeply infatuated by the vile pursuit as were their elders." It was said that a woman from the mid-eighteenth century "would stake her jewels, her husband's fortune, and even her honor, upon the cut of a card."

And for good reason. Elite women of the 1750s were even more bored than wealthy men, and not at all by choice. The guys were allowed to smoke a cigar and talk to each other about their latest read every once in a while (probably over a card game, but still). Women weren't permitted such indulgences. They *could* pass their time taking up nonthreatening, not-particularly-intellectual pursuits like needlepoint, playing a musical instrument, dancing, or drawing. Anything else? Unnecessary. Most wealthy women entered into arranged marriages with men who had little to no interest in monogamy. The wives spent their days managing empty houses and just sitting around stabbing a needle into stuff. In the so-called Age of Reason, "intellectual woman" was still an oxymoron.

For all their learning and sciencing and Deep Discussions, men genuinely didn't get that dancing and piano playing (which, don't get me wrong, can be an absolute blast in a party situation) were insufficient intellectual stimulation for their lady friends. One member of the British aristocracy, the Earl of Chesterfield, wrote to his son in 1748 that women should be thought of as "only children of a larger growth" because although "they have an entertaining tattle, and sometimes wit," he'd yet to meet a woman "who reasoned or acted consequentially for four-and-twenty hours together." He encouraged his son to "humour" and "flatter" them, but never to consult with them or trust them on "serious matters." Sixty-two years later, Reverend Sydney Smith would reveal, with great frustration, that the situation had barely changed. "It is not easy to imagine that there can be any just cause why a woman of forty should be more ignorant than a boy of twelve years of age," he wrote in the *Edinburgh Review*. "If there be any good in female ignorance, this (to use a very colloquial phrase) is surely too much of a good thing." (To his extreme credit, in 1810 the reverend was certain that the difference in intelligence between women and men was entirely accountable as "the difference in circumstance in which they have been placed" since he believed all people, regardless of gender, were born "precisely alike.") This was part of the great games of the mid-eighteenth century; men treated women like dumb kids and women mostly played along because the alternative was, you know, not having a place to live.

But some women weren't satisfied with being players. "Men are very imprudent to endeavor to make fools of those to whom they so much trust their honor and happiness and fortune," wrote 25-year-old Elizabeth Montagu in 1743. "[But] they know fools make the best slaves." Elizabeth had been born to the scholarly Robinson family and was raised in large part by her grandfather, a Cambridge University librarian. Unusually well read in both contemporary and classical literature (she mastered Latin, French, and Italian in addition to her native tongue), Elizabeth grew up with her parents, sister, three brothers, and a few oth-

er similarly well-educated friends in a social circle that appreciated debate and conversation between guys and gals. Sometimes
called Fidget for her lively attitude and love of dancing, Elizabeth
was nonetheless forced to conform to expectations; by age 22 she
was married to Edward Montagu, a 50-year-old member of parliament, which, as you might have guessed, was not a love match.
Elizabeth wrote that she "never saw one man that I loved" (girl,
I feel you). Happily, her husband had money and didn't stand
in the way of Elizabeth following her dreams of becoming a renowned intellect, so she ran with it.

After moving into a house in London's Mayfair district in
1750, the 32-year-old Elizabeth found that the haut ton—the
fancy folks in the city—were vastly different from the intellectual, proto-feminist environment she'd grown up in. The parties
she attended were "as if the two sexes had been in a state of war,"
she wrote, "the gentlemen ranged themselves on one side of the
room, where they talked their own talk, and left us poor ladies
to twirl our shuttles, and amuse each other, by conversing as we
could." At age 36, Elizabeth decided not to live the rest of her
days as the world wanted her to, "in female vanities" and "domestic employments, . . . measuring ribbon in a milliner's, or counting pennyworth of figs, or weighing sugar candy in a grocer's shop
all my life." Instead, thinking back to her childhood friendships,
she began to collect similarly minded aristocratic women who
were also bored to tears and sick of pretending to be too dumb to
understand philosophy. She started hosting small, literary break-
fasts with close friends; by 1760, her social events had grown to
full-on evening parties—although ones where gambling, drink-

ing, and dancing were banned. These soirées were nights for serious conversation only, and for the first time, not only were women allowed, they were running the show.

Elizabeth had two main co-conspirators in the foundation of this revolutionary social movement. First was Elizabeth Vesey, known to friends as "the Sylph" because she was so dang witty and flirty. Around the same age as Elizabeth Montagu, she was the daughter of an Irish bishop and married to her rich philandering cousin, Agmondesham Vesey (gesundheit). With her husband mostly out of the picture, no children, and a "domestic companion" who took care of her housework, she was free to read as much as she liked. When she met Elizabeth in the late 1740s, it was friend-love at first sight.

The two Elizabeths held those first salons with Frances Boscawen, another lady in both their age and social group. Frances, aka Fanny, was the daughter of a member of parliament who had, unconventionally, taken his wife's surname when they married (though less because he was progressive than because she was super rich and he wanted to be fancy by association). Raised by her extended family, some of whom were well known in literary circles—her great-uncle was John Evelyn, a proto-memoirist in the vein of Samuel Pepys—Fanny was an avid reader and letter writer with a wonderful sense of humor. At age 23, she married a navy captain, and the couple moved to London—though, as you can imagine, her husband traveled a lot, so Fanny thoughtfully sent him journals to keep him updated on her life. ("Beauty and I were never acquainted," she wrote him once of her looks. "But may I not hope, dear husband, that you will find charms in my heart."

Beauty? Never heard of her.) Also childless, Fanny fit right in to Elizabeth's girl gang, and thus she became the third hostess of the London literary society that would come to be known as the Blue Stockings.

But how, exactly, did they become known as "Blue Stockings?" We're not 100 percent sure, because, shockingly, there is some debate among scholars about the exact origins of the nickname. In his 1881 *Belgravia* article, Baker attributed the moniker to the ever-quippy Elizabeth the Sylph, who supposedly told one unfashionable guy friend to come to one of her salons "as you are, in your blue stockings," that particular color being an informal (or what you might call "for the poors") look at the time. When that dude, a great conversationalist, didn't show up one time, someone cried, "We can do nothing without the blue-stockings!" because they apparently both missed his company and still thought his socks were dorky. But later in the same article, Baker says the term might have come from a French woman who wore blue stockings to one gathering, which were actually super-fashionable in Paris, "and thereupon her English friends, who, with all their learning, were not above such feminine weaknesses, adopted this color for their nether casings." (Their nether casings!) Other scholars credit its origins to a name used for members of Oliver Cromwell's unpopular parliament in 1653 because of their affectedly plain dress. Regardless, the women of the society loved the term so much they adopted it unequivocally; it seemed to perfectly encapsulate the casual, social vibe of their events. By the end of the eighteenth century, everyone knew that a Blue Stocking was an educated woman not to be messed with.

And the Blue Stockings' salons were absolutely *fire*. "Mrs. Montagu and a few friends, Miss Boscawen and Mrs. Vesey, who, like herself, were untainted by this wolfish passion [i.e., gambling]," reported Baker in 1881, "resolved to make a stand against the universal tyranny of a custom which absorbed the life and leisure of the rich to the exclusion of all intellectual enjoyment, and, borrowing the idea from the Parisian salons … found[ed] a society in which conversation should supersede cards." The salons were attended by not only educated women like the Elizabeths and Fanny, but also some of the most famous intellectual men of the day, including writers Samuel Johnson and James Boswell, theater managers David Garrick (and his famous dancer wife, Eva Marie), painter Sir Joshua Reynolds, politicians, critics, and more. The women of the group shared a common goal: to raise awareness of women's intellectual capability and inspire better conversation by assembling a diverse group of people with a wide variety of experiences. At the peak of the salon's popularity, a single gathering could draw up to five hundred people from different intellectual and social backgrounds, all chatting together about art, philosophy, and literature (but never relationships or politics) while drinking sweet tea instead of booze.

The group never met on the same night two weeks in a row, and different hostesses had different party styles. Founder Elizabeth Montagu, aka "Queen of the Blues," liked a hierarchical, semicircular seating arrangement; the incredibly charming Sylph created a weird maze of chairs to encourage conversation. "She pushed all the small sofas, as well as chairs, pell-mell about the apartments, so as not to leave even a zig-zag of communication free from impediment," wrote Fanny, "and her greatest delight was to place the seats back to back, so that those who occupied them could perceive no more of their nearest neighbor than if the parties had been sent into different rooms." Elizabeth said watching unlikely people come together at the Sylph's salons was like watching as "the Lion sits down by the Lamb." One guest, diarist Mary Hamilton, wrote that only at the Sylph's house could you meet with "the Learned, the witty, the old & young, the grave, gay, wise & unwise, the fine bred Man & the pert coxcomb; The elegant female, the chaste Matron, the severe prude, & the pert Miss, but be it remembered that you can run no risque in Mrs. Vesey's parties of meeting with those who have no claim to respect." (The Sylph was flirtatious and charming with everyone, irrespective of gender, because sylphs gonna sylph.) Elizabeth called Fanny's hosting "polite, learned, judicious, and humble" and wrote that she was "one of the few whom an unbounded prosperity could not spoil," with "not a grain of evil in her composition."

These women did more than talk. Over the course of the 1700s, many Blue Stockings wrote and published poetry, literary criticism, pamphlets, and books (and got paid for it, too!). Elizabeth's sister, Sarah Scott, wrote a novel about a future utopia where women all live together in a shared property where all they do is learn things and live without men. And though the women didn't quite know how to push their ideals into law, like the Edinburgh Seven would do a few years later, they were instrumental in changing cultural attitudes by proving that women were just as able to read, consider, criticize, and discuss "serious matters" as men.

For many Blue Stockings, claiming social independence was

a big part of their mission for equality and respect. They sought to prove that women didn't need to depend on men the way societal norms insisted they did, and that women both could and should have a say in choosing a spouse. Some Blue Stockings, like the poet Elizabeth Carter and the religious writer Hannah More, stayed unmarried; both Elizabeths, as well as the writer Hester Chapone (she wrote "conduct books," manuals on behavior that taught you how to, well, conduct yourself), managed fine when widowed. Nevertheless, some Blue Stockings were stuck in arranged marriages with spouses who were unfaithful or just never around (this being the eighteenth century and all). Artist Mary Delany was stuck with a man forty-three years her senior when she was just seventeen years old, and she felt her life had been "sacrificed"; writer Hester Thrale was forced to bear her social-climbing husband twelve kids in almost as many years. The Blue Stockings' ideal was to be able to pick men to marry whose "opinion of his wife's understanding, principles, and integrity of heart, as would induce him to exalt her to the rank of his *first* and *dearest friend*" (as Hester Chapone put it). Basically, they wanted guys who, like their female literary fellows, met the criterion of friend, the only relationship the Blue Stockings considered to be of true respect, choice, love, and equality.

As with all movements concerned with social progress, over decades the Blue Stockings and their mission inspired a harsh backlash, especially around the time that the American, French, and Haitian revolutions were popping off in the late eighteenth century. Revolutionaries across the seas were executing the rich for reasons like equality and liberty and the right to vote. The

Blue Stockings' progressivism and focus on women's education became conflated with contemporary revolutionary politics, and nothing scared conservative elites in the late 1700s more than not being elite anymore. By the time Mary Wollstonecraft (not the *Frankenstein* one, her mom, the proto-feminist writer) published her *Vindication of the Rights of Woman* in 1792, "Blue Stocking" had become a term of ridicule and the idea of an educated woman had fallen out of favor. In the name of protecting the monarchy and the Church of England, the country pulled way back on equal rights between the sexes and started to develop those strict nineteenth-century rules about the separation of spheres, assigning men to the public and women to the domestic. Like most anti-women movements, they weren't quiet about it. Plenty of men (and some women suffering from internalized misogyny) wrote about their distaste for educated women and voiced their opinions about the virtue of such ladies. Take the satirist Thomas Mathias, who in his 1797 *Pursuits of Literature* decried "unsex'd female writers [who] now instruct, or confuse, us and themselves, in the labyrinth of politics, or turn us wild with Gallic frenzy." Or Richard Polwhele, a Cornish poet and clergyman—and, according to the introduction to the University of Oxford edition of his book *The Unsex'd Females, a Poem*, a "prolific writer whose work is now largely forgotten" (burn)—who wrote

> *Survey with me, what ne'er our fathers saw,*
> *A female band despising NATURE's law,*
> *As "proud defiance" flashes from their arms,*
> *And vengeance smothers all their softer charms.*

(Note: this is the same man who wrote a poem about female botanists that suggests they were only into plants because they could learn secret sex moves from them, so . . .)

Despite these restrictions on women that marked the start of the 1800s, the Blue Stockings inspired the next generation of women intellectuals and writers—and the one after that, and the one after that. Virginia Woolf called their movement more important than the Crusades or the War of the Roses. Today, almost seven thousand letters between Elizabeth and her friends are preserved at the Huntington Library in California. One of the most famous paintings of the period, Richard Samuel's *The Nine Living Muses of Great Britain*, depicts Elizabeth and eight of her closest compatriots gathered in full Grecian dress in the midst of an important discussion, looking more like the Amazons of Themyscira than anything I've ever seen. Women have revived the term Blue Stocking for everything from college yearbook titles to a cappella group names to romance novels featuring super-nerdy Blue Stockings–inspired heroines.

The Blue Stockings Society was the first literary women's group to be taken seriously in Britain. Just as important, they founded a coalition rooted in the strengths of female friendship, support between women, and ladies encouraging other ladies to write and publish and to be their very best selves. "It is charming to think how our praises will ride about the World in every bodies pocket," wrote Elizabeth Montagu in 1777. "I do not see how we could become more universally celebrated." How about right here in this book for even more women two and a half centuries later? I think the Blue Stockings would have liked that, too. ✦

Salomé Ureña and the Instituto de Señoritas

THE REVOLUTIONARY WOMEN WRITERS OF THE DOMINICAN

1881–1936

The first national poet of the Dominican Republic is probably not the kind of person you'd first picture. It's not a white-bearded bespectacled philosopher, not a balding absent-minded professor, not even a suit-jacket-wearing ascot-twirling dude with a rich dad. It's not, in fact, a man at all. The first national poet of the Dominican Republic was a woman named Salomé Ureña, and she—with a small group of brassy girlfriends—changed the face of education for women in their country forever.

Salomé was born at six in the morning on October 21, 1850, in the city of Santo Domingo in the Dominican Republic. Just six years earlier, the island nation had fought and won a bloody independence war with neighboring Haiti after more than two decades of occupation. When the Haitians took control in 1822, they didn't exactly foster a spirit of unity and cohesion between the two countries; instead, they instituted high taxes, mandatory military service, and French as the official language (instead of Spanish). This was a variation of colonialism at work: see, when the Europeans "found" the island Hispaniola in colonial times, the French ended up with the western side of the island (Haiti), and the Spanish with the east (the Dominican). Haiti had to literally buy back its independence from France in the early nineteenth century for one hundred and fifty million francs (the French were kind enough to reduce that ask to just ninety million francs, which is only about forty *billion* US dollars today) and then promptly took over the Dominican Republic and demanded money from them. So Haiti was in extreme ridiculous debt— and what better way to get your hands on a little bit of extra cash than taking over another country and demanding it from them? A few years before Salomé's birthday, on February 27, 1844, the revolutionary Juan Pablo Duarte had led the Dominican people to independence, but change was slow and fights with Haitians and the fear of another takeover were pervasive in the newly established democratic Dominican Republic of Salomé's youth.

Postwar rebuilding notwithstanding, the Dominican (like most places in 1850) was a difficult place to be a girl with dreams. Salomé's family was not rich by any means, but they were fairly well known among the Dominican intelligentsia; her mother's family owned land, and her father was a lawyer, poet, and politician who founded a newspaper called *El Progreso* in 1853. Despite some western-racism-influenced whitewashing in most portraits and statues of Salomé today, an original daguerreotype (read: old-timey photo) kept mostly hidden in a Cuban archive for decades shows that she was likely a mixed-race woman of color, with some African heritage. (Like they'd done in most of the Caribbean and the Americas, the Spanish had brought African slaves to the Dominican after European disease nearly wiped out the island's native Taíno population.) Salomé's mother taught her to read when she was 4, and Salomé attended the only two elementary schools open to girls. Beyond the basics of grammar school, no further educational options existed for girls in the Dominican of the mid-nineteenth century (lest learning be harmful for the delicate lady brain, and so on and so forth.)

Her parents had split when she was very young—after the war of independence, marriages only had to be registered with the state and not with the church, so divorce even back then was relatively simple for women. Fortunately, Salomé's father remained dedicated to her education and her future, taking up the position of teacher himself. In 1861, while the Dominican was being reannexed to Spain in the hopes of staving off another Haitian takeover, 11-year-old Salomé began a daily, customized dad-riculum of not only the classics of Spanish literature, but also French and English texts, math, and botany. These lessons included Salomé's first introduction to poetry, and she immediately fell in love. When back at her mom's house, Salomé lived with her aunt, a kindergarten teacher, who also taught Salomé on the side. By the time Salomé turned 15 in 1865, she had memorized whole poems by the sixteenth-century friar Fray Luis de León and eighteenth- and nineteenth-century priest Juan Nicasio Gallego.

That same year, the Dominican regained independence after five years of bloody conflict resisting the Spanish recolonization, and over the next three years, the Dominican was ruled by five different presidents—and all the while Salomé just kept listening and learning. Her family's social circle included the best and brightest in the country, which furthered her education.

One of her favorite family friends was Josefa Perdomo, the first published Dominican woman poet, and she may have influenced Salomé, who secretly started writing her own poetry. Not just about the things women were supposed to write about, if they wrote at all, like domestic and family matters. No, Salomé was sharp and worldly and proud to be a citizen of the DR. Her writing reflected that. Her poems were about patriotism and peace and nationhood and what she wanted to see the Dominican become. At just 17 years old, under the popular female pseudonym Herminia (a nickname that basically equated to "an anonymous woman" in literary convention), Salomé had her first poem published in a Santo Domingo newspaper. The nationalist and literati circles immediately loved her—though some older men suspected Salomé was the writer and expressed suspicion that the poems had in fact been written by her father. As she continued to publish (still anonymously), Salomé found that her writing spoke deeply to a Dominican people dreaming for hope, stability, and democracy; her words motivated and offered promise and were reprinted in foreign papers and graffitied onto Santo Domingo buildings (since Instagram wasn't a thing yet). Take the first lines of her poem "A la Patria" (To the Homeland), which are the most patriotic:

Desgarra, Patria mía, el manto que vilmente
sobre tus hombros puso la bárbara cueldad;
levanta ya del polvo la ensangrentada frente,
y entona el himno santo de unión y libertad.

In English, this translates to, "O my country, tear off that cloak that the barbarous place put on your shoulders, pick up your bloody forehead from the dust, and sing the holy hymn of unity and freedom." What Salomé wanted her country to be, so did the majority of Dominicans, and her work was blowing up.

In 1874, 24-year-old Salomé was growing tired of hiding behind a pen name; in addition, another random writer had published a fluffy article about French clothes in a Dominican newspaper under the name Herminia, which kind of tainted her pseudonymous rep. With her family's support, Salomé republished ten of her Herminia poems under her real name in the first anthology of Dominican poetry, the *Lira de Quisqueya*—poems that incorporated themes of empowerment and enfranchisement for women in a developing Dominican Republic. Salomé knew she'd been lucky with her upbringing, surrounded by intelligent and status-quo-disturbing women, and she wanted to encourage girls around her to live a similar life, both for their own benefit and for the benefit of the country. After all, a developed nation that doesn't bother to work with or listen to over half of its population isn't much of a developed nation, right? From there, Salomé's fame only increased. At age 28, Salomé received a medal for public service from the Sociedad de Amigos del Pais (Society of the Friends of the Country), becoming the Dominican's first national poet—before any man or any white woman. (In fact, this would make her the only nonwhite woman in the Americas in the 1800s to receive such an honor.)

By the time she turned thirty in 1880, Salomé had published more than thirty poems, their contents spanning from her love of progress, to the necessity of youth action in politics, to friends she'd never see again because of her beloved country's constant state of war. That year, she married one of her tutors, Francisco Henríquez y Carvajal, and published her first and only book of poetry, *Poesías* (Poems). The book included thirty-three short poems and one long one. "Ruinas" finds Salomé contemplating "the beautiful history of a former luminous age" while looking at ruins in Santo Domingo. "La fe en el porvenir" (Faith in the Future) encourages women's education and advocates for its necessity in nation building, with lines like "yours is the struggle of the ill-fated present / yours will be the future's glory." The long poem, "Anacaona," may be her best-known. It tells the story of Anacaona, the female Taíno *cacica*, or chief, who helped rule Kiskeya (the Taíno name for Hispaniola) until Christopher Columbus showed up and hanged her for trying to kick the Spanish out of her homeland. Anacaona is an *indianista*-style poem, that is, one that paints a picture of the Dominican's potential future by looking to its precolonial past and emphasizes the importance of women ruling the country. (Salomé did not pull her punches.)

Salomé and Francisco had four kids together, three of whom survived to adulthood. Her publishing slowed significantly after she became a mother, probably due to a combination of the pressures of parenting, frequent illness and "profound melancholy," and her frustration at the Meriño government, the Dominican's dictatorial leadership at the time. (One law under this regime stated that anyone even said to own a gun would be immediately killed.) She'd also taken on her most challenging task yet. A year earlier, through Francisco, she'd met a newcomer to the DR named Eugenio María de Hostos, a Puerto Rican educator who came to the Dominican to open the first "normal school" (a secular teachers college for men, basically, and he'd faced the anger of the Dominican Catholic church for it, too). Salomé watched Eugenio work on his vision and thought the school was a great idea, but a little too exclusionary. How would the girls of the progressive Dominican Republic of her dreams be responsible citizens without an education? And how would they get an education if there were no teachers to help them learn? And how could such teachers exist if there was no teacher's college for them at all?

So Salomé created her own. After two years of hard work developing a curriculum and securing support and funding (despite Salomé and Francisco's constant financial difficulties), on November 3, 1881, Salomé threw open the doors to the Instituto de Señoritas (Young Women's Institute) on *la calle de la Esperanza* (Hope Street—seriously!). The institute would become the first higher-ed school for women in the Dominican. In a country with a tyrannical leader and constantly at war, fourteen gals enrolled that first year, tossing aside cultural and religious expectations. (In this still very Spanish-influenced and Catholic-centric country, women were expected to be as domestic as possible.) Almost six years later, on April 7, 1887, the Instituto saw its first graduating class of six amazing women. These ladies had relied on one another through their studies and were now solidly friends for life: Mercedes Laura Aguiar, Ana Josefa Puello, Altagracia Henríquez Perdomo, Leonor María Feltz, Catalina F. Pou de Arvelo, and Luisa Ozema Pellerano Castro. These women comprised one of the raddest, yet least well-known, nineteenth-century squads; they were all strong writers and fiercely patriotic, following in their mentor's footsteps. For their graduation ceremony, Salomé wrote and recited a special poem, "Mi ofrenda a la patria" (My offering to the nation), which was a celebration of women's education. She spoke of the graduates as the first bastion of a new era for the Dominican, where a nation of educated women, the true holders of virtue and science, could come together to effect change for the better.

All six of these gals would end up widely published in social justice poetry and prose (especially in the renowned magazine *Letras y ciencias* [Letters and Science]), but each did her own fantastic thing. Leonor, the brains of the operation said to have "vast intelligence," taught classes first out of her home and then at Liceo Dominicano, a teachers college founded by Emilio Prud'Homme, the writer and educator who in 1883 penned the lyrics to the Dominican national anthem. Catalina was put in charge of a classroom at one of the country's two elementary schools for girls, El Dominicano, and continued the tradition of ladies getting ladies educated. So did Altagracia, who (after marrying an obstetrician named Rodolfo Coiscou Carvajal) started her own coed primary school in Santa Domingo's Villa de San Carlos district. Ana—especially close buds with Luisa, who called her "Ana Jó"—was the oldest of the bunch (the others jokingly called her "the Dean") founded El Jardín de la Infancia (the Infant Garden), a coed school that became the most respected primary school in Santo Domingo. She taught there for sixty years and was described by her students as proud, tolerant, and kind, with a "melodious voice." Ana was also a great hostess of many of the Dominican's intelligentsia and, of course, stayed in touch with her friends. Letters between the gals show that Mercedes, Luisa, and Ana in particular remained close friends, even taking care of each other when sick.

Mercedes, probably the most famous of this impressive bunch, taught for over thirty years but is best known as a feminist poet who advocated for women's suffrage, education, and workplace rights. As a founder of the women's group Sociedad Amantes de la Luz (Lovers of the Light of Day) and member of the Junta Patriótica de Damas (Board of Patriotic Ladies), Mercedes became a vocal opponent of the US occupation of the Dominican Republic in 1916. She remained active until the 1940s, when she was appointed to government lobby groups that promoted Dominican women's rights.

Finally, there was Luisa. Her life had been touched so deeply by the Instituto de Señoritas; the friendships she had formed there had such an impact on her life, and her sister Eva graduated the following year. When the Instituto shut down in 1893, Luisa and Eva were devastated. But, following Salomé's example, and with the support of friends, they knew what they had to do. With two third-year grads, Anacaona Moscoso and Lucila de Castro; two second-year grads, Mercedes M. Echenique y Pelaez and Encarnacion Suazo; and Luisa's old pal Mercedes, they reopened the

Instituto in January 1897, three months before Salomé passed away. That September, they made one small change: the school would from then on be known as the Instituto Salomé Ureña.

Salomé had made huge sacrifices to start the Instituto, serving as both teacher and principal from when she founded the school at 31 until she turned 43, even single-momming it during the four years Francisco spent in France getting his medical degree. The Instituto trained future teachers but expanded to include kindergarten, elementary, and primary school classes for younger girls, too. During her tenure, Salomé matriculated countless girls who went on to form the backbone of the next generation of Dominican writers, poets, and scholars. Finances and tuberculosis forced her retirement and the school's closure in 1893 (as TB tends to do). She died on March 6, 1897, and her funeral turned into a three-day period of mourning and celebration of her life. When people flooded the streets to remember Salomé, the impromptu demonstration became the first Dominican civic march that included women.

By the time the Instituto Salomé Ureña closed its doors in 1936, over three hundred Dominican women had walked the floor proudly at graduation. And Salomé is hardly forgotten: a secondary school still bears her name, a fictionalized history of her life was written and published by acclaimed novelist Julia Alvarez in 2000, and statues and busts of her likeness watch over school playgrounds across the DR to this day. Salomé's family—as well as the families of those six OG grads—dominated the Dominican cultural scene for the next century; their descendants are still making waves as doctors, lawyers, writers, professors, and poets around the world.

As for Francisco, after teaching at the Instituto, he would go on to be just, you know, the president of the Dominican in July 1916, serving for just a few months before the Americans arrived and began an eight-year occupation. Salomé and Francisco's oldest child, Pedro, republished his mother's poems in 1920 (conspicuously and hilariously leaving out one poem called "Amor y anhelo," which is basically about how horny Salomé is for Francisco). Her other son, Max, became a professor and diplomat. And their daughter, Camila, earned several PhDs in philosophy and pedagogy, studying everywhere from Havana to the Sorbonne before teaching at Vassar College and becoming an advocate for women's rights in Cuba.

In her way-too-short life, Salomé saw twenty-three different governments come and go in the Dominican, but she never lost her passion for the ideal of the country she believed in. Her work at the Instituto not only inspired the school's first six graduates, but also paved the way for every girl who has received an education in the Dominican Republic since the turn of the twentieth century. And, maybe most importantly of all, Salomé, Mercedes, Ana, Altagracia, Leonor, Catalina, and Luisa all believed that the pen truly was mightier than the sword, that words could change war to wisdom, that poetry may be the only thing that can unite a troubled, turbulent nation. In Camila's own words: "The arrival of women, of half of humanity to culture, is one of the greatest revolutions of our era of revolutions. And that is an indisputable and indestructible historical fact." Of that we have no better proof than the women of the Instituto de Señoritas. ✦

The Zohra Orchestra

*THE FIRST ALL-GIRL MUSICAL ENSEMBLE
IN AFGHANISTAN*

ACTIVE 2014–PRESENT

The date is January 20, 2017. At 6:30 p.m., a 16-year-old girl sits
on stage with her violin resting on her knee. She wipes a sweaty
palm on her dress and looks up at her conductor—another girl,
close to her in age—who raises her baton. The violin comes up,
tucks snugly under her chin; the bow rests on the strings, waiting for the conductor's signal to pull down and sound the first
note. A mix of nerves and excitement fills her belly as she looks
out into the darkness of the audience. She knows people are out
there, watching her and the other girls in the orchestra. They've
been practicing a long time for this. And they're ready.

So what's so remarkable about this? A similar scene probably plays out over and over again in cities around the world, from
professional concert halls to auditoriums full of middle-schoolers
in uncomfortable white shirts and black dress pants (and camera-

wielding parents ready to embarrass them). Girls playing in a school band is nothing special. Right?

Right. Unless those girls are from Afghanistan, where girls are rarely allowed to attend school, let alone music school, and where *all* music was banned for years. Where a girl has never before held a conductor's baton. The ensemble onstage on this January evening is Zohra, the first all-girls orchestra from Afghanistan; the performance, in Davos-Klosters, Switzerland, is the closing concert of the forty-seventh annual meeting of the World Economic Forum, in front of two thousand world leaders. And they're about to make every person in the room cry.

Music has been an integral part of the culture of Afghanistan since the nation, then known as Khorasan, was officially established in 1747. Most major social and cultural events in Afghan culture, like births and weddings, feature some kind of musical element (funerals are the only exception). In fact, many of the early amirs (later "emirs"), or rulers, of Kabul, the country's capital and largest city, were renowned patrons of music, and musical rivalries between different courts constantly generated innovative genres and talented performers. Amir Sher Ali Khan, who first took the throne in 1863, famously loved music and dance; after a diplomatic trip to India, he brought North Indian singers, musicians, and dancers to serve as his permanent court entertainers. (As a sidebar, like many amirs, Sher Ali was generally a pretty progressive dude, establishing schools, factories, public buildings, new towns, the first Afghan newspaper, and a postal service, in addition to being a patron of the arts.)

Sher Ali was succeeded by a series of rulers with a similar

devotion to Afghan progressivism and music: Emir Abdur Rah-man Khan (1880–1901), who gave women the right to divorce and to own property; Emir Habibullah Khan (1901–19), who opened the first girls' schools; Emir Amanullah Khan (1919–29), who gave women the right to choose their own husbands, and whose wife, Queen Soraya, firmly supported social reform for women and founded the first Afghan women's journal; and King Mohammed Zahir Shah (1933–73), who gave women the vote, helped begin Radio Kabul, and awarded singer Farida Mahwash the title of Ustad, or master, musician. In 1973, when Moham-med Daoud Khan seized the country in a coup and declared himself president, these initiatives continued; he supported women's choice in veiling and was in power when the feminist activist Meena Kamal founded the Revolutionary Association of the Women of Afghanistan. In short, for centuries, the sight and sound of both women and men playing music, in public or in the home, was a part of daily life for people in Afghanistan.

But after Daoud Khan was assassinated in 1978 by the so-cialist People's Democratic Party of Afghanistan, women's rights and civil liberties took a nosedive. The mujahideen, a US-backed Islamic guerilla resistance fighting against communist interven-tion, clashed with Soviet forces in a long and drawn-out conflict until officially taking control of the country in 1992. By 1996, the Taliban, a fundamentalist faction of Sunni Muslims, were in charge, and would remain in power until 2001. Though this civil war in the '90s had made the fight for social justice and civ-il rights increasingly difficult, the Taliban's strict interpretation of Islamic law made it almost impossible for both women and musicians in Afghanistan to live and play the way they once had. Women were banned from education and employment—they couldn't even leave the house unless they were fully covered by a burqa and accompanied by a male chaperone, including when seeking treatment from (male) doctors. Women's voices weren't permitted on the radio, and images of women were banned both in public and at home (as in, you couldn't even have a snapshot of a female family member in your living room). Any violation of these mandates resulted in public beatings or executions. And during the civil war, the mujahideen, who viewed cultural life as a constant funeral for all those who died during the conflict, banned music in Afghan refugee camps, deeming it inappropriately celebratory. Simultaneously and similarly, the communists had started bringing music under the control of the Ministry of Information and Culture; by 1992, though music was technically legal, it was subject to a ton of restrictions: musicians had to be male, had to have a license to perform, and could only play songs that venerated Islam or the government according to the tight regulations set out by the Committee for the Propagation of Virtue and the Prevention of Vice. When the Taliban came to power, they banned music entirely (which was reminiscent of the ban on music imposed by 1700s English and American Quakers), destroying cassettes, jailing musicians, and sometimes beating performers with their own instruments. In a very short time, the once-vibrant music of Afghanistan had been silenced.

Since the US-Afghanistan war began in 2001, two presidents have been elected in Afghanistan, and they've attempted to push back against the influence of the Taliban in the hopes of reinstating personal freedoms and rights for women. But it's been challenging, especially in a country where generations of families have been taught that women belong in the home and that music is frivolous at best and an instrument of evil at worst. It was in this environment that, in 2010, Dr. Ahmad Naser Sarmast, with the help of the Ministry of Education, reopened the Afghanistan National Institute of Music (ANIM) in Kabul, which was originally founded in 1974 as part of the national curriculum.

The son of the first Afghan man ever to conduct a symphony orchestra, Ahmad received his bachelor and master degrees in music in Russia, and, when he was unable to return to his war-torn homeland, became the first Afghan to receive a PhD in music while living under asylum in Australia. He returned to Afghanistan after the Taliban was removed from power, and with World Bank funding in 2008, he began the Reconstruction of the Afghan Music program, out of which sprung ANIM in 2010. ANIM students learn music on top of receiving a general education, and the school's goal is to provide "a dynamic, challenging, and safe learning environment for all students regardless of their gender, ethnicity, religious sect, or socio-economic circumstances." ANIM focuses on the most marginalized kids in Afghanistan: orphans, street vendors, and girls. Ahmad strongly believes that music is integral in healing a country torn apart by war, in rebuilding and revitalizing Afghan culture, and in honoring the country's heritage while educating and improving its next generation. "These children benefit not only from the proven therapeutic capabilities of music in easing trauma and grief," said Ahmad in his ANIM mission statement, "but also in developing a vocation that will sustain them professionally and economical-ly while contributing to the rebuilding of musical and cultural traditions." Of ANIM's 250 students from provinces across Af-ghanistan—the first students to study music in the country in thirty years—a remarkable seventy-five are girls.

In 2014, four years after ANIM was established, one of Ah-mad's students, a trumpet player named Meena, came to him with a special request: she and some friends wanted to form an all-girl ensemble, something that Afghanistan had never seen. Ah-mad, dedicated to furthering girls' education and excited about the potential of the new styles and songs that could come out of their efforts, was on board right away. According to Ahmad, they decided to call their new orchestra Zohra, after a Persian goddess of music. Over the last decade, the orchestra has grown from five to thirty-five members, ranging from 12 to 21 years of age. Twice-weekly rehearsals are included in the girls' education at ANIM, and they learn to read music (an amazing feat considering that just 22 percent of Afghan women are literate at all) and to play not only Western music on instruments like the violin, viola, piano, and flute, but also Afghan music on traditional stringed instruments similar to the lute or the sitar, including the rubab, qashquarcha, ghaychak, sarod, and dilruba. When they started at ANIM, most of these girls couldn't even name a traditional Afghan instrument. Pretty impressive stuff.

Zohra's existence "shows just what can be achieved when a young girl walks into an office, clearly asks for what she wants, and is the given the opportunity," reads the ANIM website. "The idea of one young girl can not only transform the lives of many of her friends, but also transform the international perception of her country and bring increased awareness to women's rights issues." Even more impressive: Zohra is led and conducted by two young girls, 20-year-old Negin Khpalwak and 18-year-old Zarifa Adiba, the first female conductors in the country. After its founding, Zohra played its very first event at the Canadian Embassy in Kabul, and the group has only continued to improve.

Which is why, in December 2014, Ahmad was excited to attend an ANIM performance at one of Kabul's cultural centers. It was a play about the possibilities of new life after terrorism. When he noticed the lights flickering, Ahmad reached for his phone to make sure nothing was wrong—and in one of the most fortunate clumsy moves ever made, he dropped it. Bending over to pick up his phone saved Ahmad's life, shielding his head from the worst of the blast created by a teenage suicide bomber just rows behind him, sent by the Taliban to target Ahmad for his work at ANIM. He was airlifted to Australia, had nine pieces of shrapnel removed from his skull, and lost his hearing in one ear.

Three months later, he was back teaching at ANIM.

Of course Ahmad, who has said that the Taliban brainwashed a generation of Afghan people, is not the only person at ANIM who lives under the constant threat of violence. "When I have my musical instruments with me, people talk a lot behind my back," Meena, the trumpeter and Zohra founder, told Reuters in 2016. After she took what was supposed to be a short leave in April 2016 to attend her sister's wedding in Jalalabad, where her mother is a policewoman, the school lost contact with her. A year and a half later, she called ANIM to tell them she was safe and wanted to return one day. "Most of the girls come from the provinces where girl's education doesn't have strong support," Ahmad told *Huck Magazine* in 2017. "The fathers of the families are generally very supportive of their kids but they are giving in to pressure from the religious leader of their village or a member of their clan."

That's been the case for both of Zohra's conductors. Negin was born in northeastern Afghanistan in 1997, in a Pashtun village with no schools that, like many communities in the country, is largely controlled by senior Islamic clerics called *mullahs* who deemed Negin's musicianship *haram* (forbidden under religious law). Only one person supported her dream: "Apart from my father, everybody in the family is against it," Negin told Reuters. "They say, 'How can a Pashtun girl play music?' Especially in our tribe, where even a man doesn't have the right to do it." The *mullahs* told her to stay home and clean. Pushing back against her grandmother, who feared the shame she would bring down on the family and who threatened to disown her, and her brothers and uncles, who have threatened to beat and kill her on multiple occasions, Negin's father escaped with her to Kabul, installing her at the Afghan Child Education and Care Organization orphanage, a facility close to the school where many ANIM students board for their safety. "I lost every member of my family, except my father," Negin told *Huck Magazine*, matter-of-factly describing something that happened when she wasn't yet 10 years old. "It was so hard for me, but I love music so I am continuing this way."

After studying the traditional stringed sarod, the piano, percussion instruments, and singing, Negin decided to break new ground once again and learn to conduct an ensemble, making her the first gal conductor in her country's history. She finds leadership an enjoyable challenge, and at concerts she calms her nerves by focusing on the smiles of the girls in front of her. Negin knows her dreams can be dangerous: "The people in our province, they're always saying that whenever we see you, we will kill you," Negin told CBS News in 2017. But she also knows that her efforts make it easier for the girls after her to pick up a pen or a bow or a flute. "If we stay in the home, the new generation will also stay in the home. If we open the door for other generations, it will be good." So she doesn't allow herself to be scared for long. "I am not that Negin anymore," she told Reuters. "I will never accept defeat. I will continue to play music. I do not feel safe, but when people see me and say, 'That is Negin Khpalwak,' that gives me energy."

Following in Negin's baton-slashing footsteps is Zarifa Adiba, only two years younger than Negin. Zarifa—who doesn't talk about her ethnicity, describing herself to NPR in 2017 as "Afghan—and before being Afghan, I'm Muslim, and before being Muslim, I'm human"—first dreamed of being a pop star as a refugee in Pakistan, where she sang every day. After being forced back to the Taliban-controlled province of her birth in 2014, only her mother and her stepfather supported her ninth-grade enrollment at ANIM; her uncles strongly opposed it. She remembers her mother telling her "what you love, go ahead and find out." Zarifa started playing the flute but was soon attracted to the more offbeat and less popular viola: "[It] was so attractive to me," Zarifa told NPR. "There was just one boy and one girl playing the viola and I said I wanted to be the second girl playing viola." She picked up the conductor's baton shortly after and hasn't looked back since.

After years of practice and publicity, in 2016 the Zohra orchestra received an invitation they could never have dreamed of. The members of the World Economic Forum wanted the ensemble to perform at their closing ceremonies in Switzerland, just after the new year, as part of a twenty-day, eleven-concert, five-city European tour for the girls. Ahmad worked tirelessly to ensure the girls would be able to get there, securing funding from an Italian bank and other European partners, having parents sign permission slips, and pushing through the complex visa process with European countries that were scared the girls would try to seek asylum. Meanwhile, Negin and Zarifa arranged extra rehearsals and ran the girls tirelessly through Afghan songs, Western pieces, and even a special arrangement of Beethoven's Ninth Symphony. On top of all that, in preparation for their time in Weimar and Berlin, the Zohra girls took German lessons so they could be not only multi-instrumental but multilingual as well. On the flip side, youth orchestras in Switzerland and Germany began learning about Afghan culture and music—especially its 7/8 time signature—to prep for playing with Zohra.

By December 2016, against all odds, all the necessary funding, permissions, and travel plans were in place. On January 13, Ahmad and the girls of Zohra took their first flight, from Kabul to Dubai, and then flew on to Weimar, Germany, after a six-hour layover. The boys and girls of the German youth orchestra were so excited to meet and tour with them, getting to rehearse together IRL for the first time. From Weimar, the girls of Zohra traveled by bus to Davos for the WEF concert (which you can and absolutely should watch on YouTube). One video of the trip shows Ahmad and the girls sitting around a table, laughing at a Facebook comment about the orchestra: "Music is the job of Satan, and they are the spawn, and what you do is the job of Satan." Ahmad translates, still laughing. "Ninety-nine percent of the Afghan people are behind us. Who cares about these one-percent, narrow-minded, ignorant people?"

Zohra arrived in Davos at night, all the girls wearing matching coats; the temperature there was twenty-three degrees Fahrenheit colder than in Kabul, and the girls were battling jet lag and dehydration. They ate dinner with the youth orchestra from Geneva that would be performing with them and turned in for the night. The next day, reporters from across the globe were waiting to speak with Negin, Zarifa, and Ahmad—not only the BBC and NPR and NBS, but also TOLOnews, Afghanistan's national television station broadcast out of Kabul. Before an audience of thousands of world leaders, the ladies of Zohra took the stage, dressed to the nines in bright, colorful dresses and embroidered headscarves, many in green, red, and black, the colors of the Afghan flag. While Zohra played, Donald Trump was taking the oath of office as President of the United States on the other side of the globe, but Zohra's audience was both more impressive and undoubtedly more impressed.

Following their incredible debut on the world stage, Zohra played a sold-out show in Zurich, followed by six concerts in freezing-cold Geneva. The girls were exhausted, but they still cheered whenever they saw an ad for their performances, and they were even more excited when first violinist Marjan accepted the Freemuse Award, a prize given annually to a person or group working for musical freedom of expression, on behalf of the orchestra. Next, Zohra traveled to Berlin, where, just six weeks earlier, an ISIL terrorist had driven a truck into a Christmas market, killing twelve people. Aware that their tour could be subject to the same kind of extremist violence, the girls were not deterred. They performed a free show at Kaiser Wilhelm Memorial Church, a World War II memorial building, and dedicated their performance to the victims of the recent attack. Ahmad said that he hoped Zohra's performance would help to "wash away with the beauty of music the blood spilled on the streets of Berlin." The next morning, the girls visited a zoo for the first time. Their last performance was back in Weimar, and they boarded their planes to Kabul, not knowing what would be waiting for them back home.

Fortunately for all, it was love. As they deplaned at the Hamid Karzai International Airport, they found a crowd of hundreds waiting to greet them, some bearing flowers, some clamoring for interviews, and many offering congratulations. Zarifa, the conductor and violist whose music was barely tolerated before she left home, was met by her uncles, who told her that they had been wrong. Now they were proud.

Through their music, the girls of Zohra have spread a message of peace and tolerance the world over, exposing a side of Afghanistan that the Western world rarely gets to see. Afghanistan is still in turmoil, and the Taliban is fighting every day to take back power. Amnesty International consistently reports increased incidence of violence against women, many of whom are simply trying to just get to work or school. But the girls of Zohra are positive that their movement and their message can help build a better future for Afghan women. "I'm happy that at least I changed my family," Zarifa told NPR. "[Other girls] are going to change their families and when their families are going to change, you can have a society which is changed." She's served as a youth ambassador for Australia's Bridge the Divide initiative, attended Yale's Young Global Scholars program, and participated in the Youth Solidarity and English Language program in Turkey. She wants to become a lawyer to defend the rights of artists in Afghanistan. Negin has represented Afghan music in Turkmenistan, the UAE, and the US and became the first Afghan girl to publicly perform on the sarod in 2013. She hopes to continue her music training so that she can create and lead an Afghan national symphony orchestra.

Ahmad hopes to introduce music to every school curriculum in Afghanistan but knows doing so is going to be a slow process. Western educators and donations are key to keeping ANIM afloat, especially since they subsidize living costs of students at the orphanage. "Afghanistan needs, more than anything else, to benefit from the healing power of music," he told the BBC. "And our students—yes, they're living in a tough environment. There's a lot of pressure, a lot of concern about their security and safety. But at the end of the day it's music which makes them very strong and gives them hope for the future and allows them to be the wonderful role model for other young Afghan girls."

Orchestral music inherently requires more than one person to make sound, to make a difference. And the Zohra Orchestra gets that on so, so many levels. Zohra shows the power of the orchestra *as a group,* as a place for girls to unite and make art and feel a sense of belonging and happiness, to the billionth degree. As Zarifa wrote for *Pavlovic Today* in 2017, ANIM "is the only place where all of us can smile from the depths of our hearts. Where we feel just as safe as we would anywhere else in the world." You simply *can't* have an orchestra without that sense of belonging (or, you can, but it's going to sound kind of terrible) and the fact that these ladies made it happen in the face of forces determined to keep music, and women's music in particular, verboten, is beyond impressive. Zarifa. Negin. Sunbul, Shugufa, Anita, Taranum, Wajia, Sahar, Ahmad, Samia, Swinj, Wajiya, Nazira, Gul-mina, Marjan, Gulalay, Lauren, Madina, Shaperay, Maram, Marzia, Aziza, Kreshma, Shukria, Mozhgan, Rabia, Mina: every one of these women and girls is needed to make the Zohra, and its music, complete.

But they won't be the last. Fifty more students join ANIM's ranks every year. Zohra's newest and youngest member is Mena Karimi, just 13 years old, who told New Delhi's *LiveMint* in December 2017 that Negin is her role model. "I am learning music in order to help other children of my age and those younger than me. I want to set the example to show them that music is good, there is nothing wrong with learning music and it brings opportunities," said Mena. "Music is my life. ✦

Selected Bibliography

For a complete list of references consulted, including primary sources, please visit http://www.quirkbooks.com/girlsquads.

CHAPTER ONE: ATHLETE SQUADS

THE HAENYEO

"Culture of Jeju Haenyeo (women divers)." UNESCO Intangible Cultural Heritage list. http://ich.unesco.org/en/RL/culture-of-jeju-haenyeo -women-divers-01068.

DenHoed, Andrea. "The Sea Women of South Korea." *New Yorker*, March 29, 2015.

Sang-hun, Choe. "Hardy Divers in Korea Strait, 'Sea Women' Are Dwindling." *New York Times*, March 29, 2014.

SHIRLEY AND SHARON FIRTH

Firth, Sharon. "First indigenous women inducted into Canada's Sports Hall of Fame." Interview by Carol Off. *As It Happens*, CBC Radio, October 21, 2015.

Meili, Dianne. "Shirley Firth-Larsson: quiet, accomplished and inspiring others to the end." *Windspeaker* 31, no. 3 (2013): 22.

O'Bonsawin, Christine M. "The Construction of the Olympian Firth Sisters by the Canadian Press." In *The Global Nexus Engaged: Sixth International Symposium for Olympic Research*, edited by Kevin B. Wamsley, Robert K. Barney, and Scott G. Maryn, 193–98. University of Western Ontario, October 2002.

THE 1964 JAPANESE WOMEN'S VOLLEYBALL TEAM

Macnaughtan, Helen. "An interview with Kasai Masae, captain of the Japanese women's volleyball team at the 1964 Tokyo Olympics." *Japan Forum* 24, no. 4 (2012): 491–500.

———. "The Oriental Witches: Women, Volleyball and the 1964 Tokyo Olympics." *Sport in History* 34 no. 1 (2014): 134–56.

———. *Women, Work and the Japanese Economic Miracle: The case of the cotton textile industry, 1945–1975*. London: RoutledgeCurzon, 2005.

Whiting, Robert. "'Witches of the Orient' symbolized Japan's fortitude." *Japan Times*, October 21, 2014.

MADISON KEYS AND SLOANE STEPHENS

Baggett, David, and Neil Delaney Jr. "Friendship, Rivalry, and Excellence." In *Tennis and Philosophy: What the Racket Is All About*, edited by David Baggett, 255–73. Lexington: University Press of Kentucky, 2010.

Brennan, Christine. "In U.S. Open final, Sloane Stephens, Madison Keys show true meaning of friendship." *USA Today*, September 9, 2017.

Keating, Steve. "Preview: Tennis: Madison Keys, Sloane Stephens put friendship to Grand Slam test." *Reuters*, September 10, 2017.

———. "Slams come and go, Keys and Stephens friendship remains." *Reuters*, September 9, 2017.

CHAPTER TWO: POLITICAL & ACTIVIST SQUADS

TRƯNG TRẮC AND TRƯNG NHỊ

Gilbert, Marc Jason. "When Heroism is Not Enough: Three Women Warriors of Vietnam, Their Historians and World History." *World History Connected* 4, no. 3 (June 2007).

Lee, Johnathan, H. X., and Kathleen M. Nadeau, eds. *Encyclopedia of Asian American Folklore and Folklife* vol. 1, 1214, 1238. Santa Barbara: ABC-CLIO, 2011.

Womack, Sarah. "The Remakings of a Legend: Women and Patriotism in the Hagiography of the Tru'ng Sisters." *Crossroads: An Interdisciplinary Journal of Southeast Asian Studies* 9, no. 2 (1995): 31–50.

Xuyen, Ly Te. "The Trung Sisters." Translated by Brian E. Ostrowski and Brian A. Zottoli. In *Sources of Vietnamese Tradition*, edited by George E. Dutton, Jayne S. Werner, and John K. Whitmore, 56–57. New York: Columbia University Press, 2012.

MANON ROLAND AND SOPHIE GRANDCHAMP

Linton, Marisa. *Choosing Terror: Virtue, Friendship, and Authenticity in the French Revolution*. Oxford: Oxford University Press, 2013.

———. "Fatal Friendships: The Politics of Jacobin Friendship." *French Historical Studies* 31, no. 1 (Winter 2008): 51–76.

Roland, Mme. *Mémoires de Madame Roland*. Edited by Claude Perroud. Paris: Plon, 1905.

Tarbell, Ida M. "Madame Roland." *Scribner's Magazine* 14 (July–December 1893): 561–78.

THE PATRIOTIC WOMEN'S LEAGUE OF IRAN

Dawlatšāhī, Mehrangīz. "Eskandarī, Moḥtaram." *Encyclopædia Iranica* vol. VIII fasc. 6 (1998): 606–7.

Ettehadieh, Mansoureh. "The Origins and Development of the Women's Movement in Iran, 1906–41." In *Women in Iran from 1800 to the Islamic Republic*, edited by Lois Beck and Guity Nashat, 85–106. Urbana: University of Illinois Press, 2004.

Nashat, Guity. *Women and Revolution in Iran*. Boulder, CO: Westview Press, 1983.

Sedghi, Hamideh. *Women and Politics in Iran: Veiling, Unveiling, and Reveiling*. Cambridge: Cambridge University Press, 2007.

RUTH BADER GINSBURG, SONIA SOTOMAYOR, AND ELENA KAGAN

Ginsburg, Ruth Bader. *My Own Words*. New York: Simon & Schuster, 2016.

Kagan, Elena. "The Changing Faces of First Amendment Neutrality: R.A.V. v St. Paul, Rust v Sullivan, and the Problem of Content-Based Underinclusion." *Supreme Court Review* 1992 (1992): 29–77.

———. "Private Speech, Public Purpose: The Role of Governmental Motive in First Amendment Doctrine." *University of Chicago Law Review* 63, no. 2 (1996): 413–517.

Sotomayor, Sonia. "Anti-Latino discrimination at Princeton." *Daily Princetonian* 98, no. 61 (May 10, 1974): 8.

———. *My Beloved World*. New York: Vintage, 2014.

CHAPTER THREE: WARRIOR SQUADS

THE DAHOMEY AMAZONS

Alpern, Stanley B. *Amazons of Black Sparta: The Women Warriors of Dahomey*. 2nd ed. New York University Press, 2011.

———. "On the Origins of the Amazons of Dahomey." *History in Africa* 25 (1998): 9–25.

Bay, Edna G. *Wives of the Leopard: Gender, Politics, and Culture in the Kingdom of Dahomey*. Charlottesville: University of Virginia Press, 1998.

Edgerton, Robert B. *Warrior Women: The Amazons of Dahomey and the Nature of War*. Boulder, CO: Westview Press, 2000.

ANNE BONNY AND MARY READ

Johnson, Charles. *A General History of the Pyrates, from Their First Rise and Settlement in the Island of Providence, to the Present Time*. London: T. Warner, 1724.

Little, Benerson. *The Golden Age of Piracy: The Truth Behind Pirate Myths*. New York: Skyhorse, 2016.

Rediker, Marcus. "Liberty beneath the Jolly Roger: The Lives of Anne Bonny and Mary Read, Pirates." In *Iron Men, Wooden Women: Gender and Seafaring in the Atlantic World, 1700–1920*, edited by Margaret S. Creighton and Lisa Norling. Baltimore: Johns Hopkins University Press, 1996.

Woodward, Colin. *The Republic of Pirates: Being the True and Surprising Story of the Caribbean Pirates and the Man who Brought Them Down*. Orlando: Harcourt, 2007.

THE RED LANTERNS SHINING

Honglin, M. A. "Lin Hei'er." In *Biographical Dictionary of Chinese Women*, volume 1: *The Qing Period, 1644–1911*, edited by Lily Xiao Hong Lee, Clara Wing-chung Ho, and A. D. Stefanowska, 131–3. Translated by N. G. Wing Chung. Armonk, NY: M. E. Sharpe, 1998.

Lynch, George. *The War of Civilisations: Being the Record of a "Foreign Devil's" Experiences with the Allies in China*. London: Longmans, Green, and Co., 1901.

Ono, Kazuko. *Chinese Women in a Century of Revolution, 1850–1950*. Edited by Joshua A. Fogel. Translated by Kathryn Bernhardt, Timothy Brook, Joshua A. Fogel, Jonathan Lipman, Susan Mann, and Laurel Rhodes. Stanford: Stanford University Press, 1989.

Xiang, Lanxin. *The Origins of the Boxer War: A Multinational Study*. London: RoutledgeCurzon, 2003.

THE WOMEN OF THE FINNISH RED GUARD

Lintunen, Tiina. "'A Danger to the State and Society': Effects of the Civil War on Red Women's Civil Rights in Finland in 1918." In *Suffrage, Gender and Citizenship: International Perspectives on Parliamentary Reforms*, edited by Irma Sulkunen, Seija-Leena Nevala-Nurmi, and Pirjo Markkola, 177–92. Newcastle upon Tyne: Cambridge Scholars, 2009.

———. "Filthy Whores and Brave Mothers: Women in War Propaganda." In *Enemy Images in War Propaganda*, edited by Marja Vuorinen, 15–34. Newcastle upon Tyne: Cambridge Scholars, 2012.

————. "Red women's paths: The wartime activity, sentences and subsequent lives of the women from the Pori area taken to political crime courts in 1918." Doctoral thesis, University of Turku, 2015.

————. "'She Wolves and Russian Brides' – Women Enemies in War Propaganda." In *Proceedings of the 9th European Conference on Information Warfare and Security*, edited by Josef Demergis, 183–9. Reading, UK: Academic Publishing Limited, 2010.

CHAPTER FOUR: SCIENTIST SQUADS

ANANDI JOSHI, KEI OKAMI, AND SABAT ISLAMBOOLY

Dall, Caroline Healey. *The Life of Dr. Anandabai Joshee, A Kinswoman of the Pundita Ramabai*. Boston: Roberts Brothers, 1888.

Joshee, Anandibai. Anandibai Joshee to Alfred Jones, June 28, 1883. South Asian American Digital Archive, https://www.saada.org/item/20120711-721.

————. *Obstetrics Among the Aryan Hindoos*. Doctoral thesis, Women's Medical College of Pennsylvania, 1886.

Matsuda, Makoto. *Kakke o nakushita otoko Takaki Kanehiro den*. 610–23. Tokyo: Kodansha, 1990. "The Curious Students of Jikei 4: The First Female Doctor of Jikei Hospital Doctor Keiko Okami" translated by Cheridan Scott.

THE EDINBURGH SEVEN

Chaplin-Ayrton, Matilda. "Lady Medicals in Japan." *Scotsman*, May 5, 1874.

Jex-Blake, Sophia. "The Late Disturbance at Surgeons' Hall." *Scotsman*, November 21, 1870.

————. "Medical Education of Women." *Times* (London), June 20, 1874.

————. *Medical Women: A Thesis and a History*. Edinburgh: Oliphant, Anderson, & Ferrier, 1886.

Thorne, Isabel [*sic*]. "Medical Education of Women." *Times* (London), June 18, 1874.

THE WOMEN SCIENTISTS OF ANTARCTICA

Blackadder, Jesse. "Frozen Voices: Women, Silence, and Antarctica." In *Antarctica: Music, Sounds, and Cultural Connections*, edited by Bernadette Hince, Rupert Summerson, and Arnan Wiesel. Acton: Australian National University Press, 2015.

———. "Heroines of the Ice." *Australian Geographic* 113 (March–April 2013): 88–98.

Bull, Colin. "Behind the Scenes: Colin Bull Recalls His 10-Year Quest to Send Women Researchers to Antarctica." *Antarctic Sun*, November 13, 2009.

Cahoon, Sister Mary Odile. "If Women Are in Science and Science Is in the Antarctic, Then Women Belong There." In *Women in the Antarctic*, edited by Esther D. Rothblum, Jacqueline S. Weinstock, and Jessica F. Morris, 31–40. Binghampton, NY: Haworth Press, 1998.

THE WEST AREA COMPUTERS

Golemba, Beverly E. "Human Computers: The Women in Aeronautical Research." Unpublished manuscript, NASA Langley Archives, March 6, 1995. http://crgis.ndc.nasa.gov/crgis/images/c/c7/Golemba.pdf.

Harris, Duchess, Lucy Short, and Ayaan Natala. "Timeline." Human Computers at NASA. Macalester College Department of American Studies. http://omeka.macalester.edu/humancomputerproject/timeline.

Harris, Miriam Mann. "Miriam Daniel Mann bio." NASA.gov, September 12, 2011. http://crgis.ndc.nasa.gov/crgis/images/d/d3/MannBio.pdf.

McLennan, Sarah, and Mary Gainer. "When the Computer Wore a Skirt: Langley's Computers, 1935–1970." *NASA History Program Office News & Notes* 29, no. 1 (first quarter 2012): 25–32.

CHAPTER FIVE: ARTIST SQUADS

THE TROBAIRITZ

Bruckner, Matilda Tomaryn. "The Trobairitz." In *A Handbook of the Troubadours*, edited by F. R. P. Akehurst and Judith M. Davis, 201–32. Berkeley: University of California Press, 1995.

Burl, Aubrey. *Courts of Love, Castles of Hate: Troubadours and Trobairitz in Southern France 1071–1321*. Gloucestershire, UK: History Press, 2008.

Keelan, Claudia. "Do You or Don't You Love Me, Baby? Finding the Trobairitz: An Essay and Translations." *American Poetry Review* 42, no. 3 (May/June 2013): 23–29.

———. *Truth of My Songs: Poems of the Trobairitz*. Richmond, CA: Omnidawn, 2015.

THE BLUE STOCKINGS

Baker, H. Barton. "The Queen of the Blue-Stockings." Belgravia 44 (1881): 160–70.

Eger, Elizabeth. "Bluestocking circle (act. c. 1755–c. 1795)." In *Oxford Dictionary of National Biography*, edited by Sir David Cannadine. Oxford University Press, 2004; online ed., September 1, 2017.

———. *Bluestockings: Women of Reason from Enlightenment to Romanticism*. Basingstoke, England: Palgrave Macmillan, 2010.

———. "Boscawen [née Glanville], Frances Evelyn [Fanny] (1719–1805)." In *Oxford Dictionary of National Biography*, edited by Sir David Cannadine. Oxford University Press, 2004; online ed., September 23, 2004. https://doi .org/10.1093/ref:odnb/47078.

SALOME UREÑA AND THE INSTITUTO DE SEÑORITAS

Durán, Carmen. *Historia e ideología: mujeres dominicanas, 1880–1950*. Publicaciones del Archivo General de la Nación, edited by Lillibel Noemí Blanco Fernández, vol. 117. Santo Domingo: Archivo General de la Nación, 2010.

N., Héctor Tineo. "Muere la maestra Mercedes Laura Aguiar Mendoza." *Diario Dominicano*, January 1, 2017. http://www.diariodominicano.com/cultura/2017/01/01/235202/muere-la-maestra-mercedes-laura-aguiar-mendoza.

Paravisini-Gebert, Lizabeth. "Salomé Ureña de Henríquez (Dominican Republic)." In *Spanish American Women Writers: A Bio-Bibliographical Source Book*, edited by Diane E. Marting, 522–31. New York: Greenwood Press, 1990.

Ramírez, Dixa. "Salomé Ureña's Blurred Edges: Race, Gender, and Commemoration in the Dominican Republic." *Black Scholar* 45, no. 2 (2015): 45–56.

THE ZOHRA ORCHESTRA

Adiba, Zarifa. "From Bombs to the Only All-Female Zohra Orchestra in Afghanistan." *Pavlovic Today*, May 15, 2017.

Emadi, Hafizullah. *Repression, Resistance, and Women in Afghanistan*. Westport, CT: Praeger, 2002.

"Ensemble Zohra Afghan Women's Orchestra." Afghanistan National Institute of Music. http://www.anim-music.org/girls-ensemble.

"The Story of Zohra." Zohra Music website. World Economic Forum and the Afghanistan National Institute of Music. http://www.zohra-music.org.

Index

ACKNOWLEDGMENTS

My unending gratitude: to Blair Thornburgh, editrix extraordinaire, and Maria Vicente, agent *incroyable*. How great is it to get to make a book about female friendships with each other? See you in 2019.

To Brett, David, Jason, Jane, Nicole, Katherine, Kelsey, Christina, Ivy, and the Quirk crew for having me in your family. To Claire and co. at PRHC for helping to get this out to Canadians. To Andie and illustrator (and fellow Torontonian) Jenn for such a punk-rock and polished book.

To Western University (and Professor M, who still calls me his favorite student); the Toronto Reference Library and Page & Panel; Danielle Carrier, Dr. Eliza Lo Chin, and the American Medical Women's Association archives; and translators Karyn Hepburn, Anthony Langlois, Cheridan Scott, Ulla Virtanen, and Hanna Harri.

To my wickedly talented BioWare coworkers, for understanding why I could never hang. To Patrick and Karin, for adopting me as a stranger in a strange (and cold) land.

To my brilliant buds, who loved me even after I moved across the continent (did you know it's cold in Edmonton?): Elena, Karyn, Meg, Rachel, Soha, Danny, Scott, Ted, Amy, Kristin, Emma F., Fox, Tom, Stacey, Sarah I., Emma L., Steffi, Sarah W., Esti, Nikki, Regina, Sa, Ritzy, Rowan, Adri, Seb, John, Lee, Megan, Shaun, Rose, Hilary, Ann, Piper, Jill, Victoria, Ashley, Kate, Wendy, Irene, Jen, Marguerite, Sam, Ryan, Paulina, and Jeph, at a start. I would be lost without y'all.

With love to my Grandma and Staramama for telling everyone they know about my books.

Hi Mom! Hi Dad! I could thank you one million times and it still wouldn't cover everything you've done for me. Thank you for believing that I'd Make It and for all the care packages. I love you both more than words could possibly say. (Not great for a writer, I know.)

Forever thanks to my Dungeon Master (the D&D kind) and fiancé, Blair Brown. Thank you for being the Ben to my Leslie; the Perez to my Tosh; the do less to my stress. (Absolutely no thank you for making me an Oilers fan.) Let's get swole and have fun adventures and own tiny dogs together. Thanks for waiting so patiently for those cookies. I swear I'll make them soon.

And finally, to you, my amazing reader, and your gal pals. Support each other. Love each other. Resist together. And let's keep changing the world. ✦